CRAC
THE CLIENT
ATTRACTION CODE

MASTER YOUR GAME, ATTRACT YOUR IDEAL CLIENTS,
CREATE INFINITE ABUNDANCE AND PROSPERITY

Carla McNeil and Nilofer Safdar

2015

Dedication:

This book is dedicated to all our speakers for their invaluable contribution without which the book would not exist.

It is also dedicated to all the listeners of our virtual event, Best Client Summit. Your questions allowed us to go places and create more possibilities.

In gratitude, this book is dedicated to Moulana Amiruddin Saheb for always being a beacon of light in Nilofer's life.

To our parents who empowered each of us with Choice, and allowed us to soar.

To our husbands, Don and Zubair, for supporting us every step of the way.

To Nilofer's kids, Nawaz and Zain, for contributing to my life and my awareness and my business in magical and wondrous ways.
(Carla has no kids)

Foreword

Can you be a heart-centered person and a successful entrepreneur? Or is this a contradiction? Many heart-centered entrepreneurs struggle with this question. Don't charge enough for their products and services to break even. Give too much away. Feel uncomfortable marketing and selling. Believe that being heart-centered is all about loving and giving. And making money is just about "taking."

Although the answer to the question is a resounding "NO," many heart-centered would-be entrepreneurs don't believe that a successful business feels heart-centered. Some work at a day job they don't like because they can't bring themselves to sell their jewelry or their metaphysical gifts that heal people.

This book began with the dream of Carla McNeil and Nilofer Safdar to prove that heart-centered marketing isn't a contradiction. And to show both concrete marketing strategies and what they call the "inner game"—those limiting beliefs that can keep you stuck. They invited 13 heart-centered, successful marketers to the *Best Client Seminar* to present their stories, strategies and best practices.

They invited folks whose businesses focus on spirituality and wellness such as Amethyst Wyldfyre, the Empress of Empowerment to Jeff Herring, an expert at content creation and other marketing strategies. Carla and Nilofer asked each presenter just one question: What is the unique transformation you want to offer our audience?

The edited and expanded interviews from *Best Client Seminar* form the foundation of *Cracking the Client Attraction Code*.

Although the answers vary wildly depending on the personalities and expertise of individual presenters, they agree on three factors. First, that running a successful heart-centered business is possible. Second, that such a business demands integrity, being oneself, and paying attention to limiting beliefs. And third, that one must have not only expertise in the products or services being sold but also knowledge of marketing principles and strategies.

A couple of chapter that I found transforming include one by Dana Garrison who helps her clients dump unconscious beliefs that come from early childhood and family. These beliefs can zap a business before it even gets off the ground.

She explains: "Family Entanglements are the problems and patterns that are passed down from generation to generation. These patterns get passed down for up to seven generations before they fade out, and you're often most deeply affected by the last three generations. That means the relatives in your parent's generation, your grandparent's generation, and your great grandparent's generation are the ones from which you inherit the most."

I also love the tools Gary Douglas, the founder of Access Consciousness®, offers and his right-on, if quirky, way of explaining things. Ironically, I had just been introduced to his book *Money isn't the Problem, You Are* and was into re-reading it, highlighting, and turning down pages when he turned up in "Best Client Seminar."

Dana and Gary represent only two examples of the inspiration you'll find in each chapter. Don't take my favorites as the best. You'll find your own in the following pages.

As a heart-centered entrepreneur with years of study behind me in both limiting beliefs and marketing, I've found that *Cracking the Client Attraction Code* has the potential to transform your business, just as Carla and Nilofer promised. I gained insight about myself and learned some wonderful new marketing tools.

Read each chapter slowly. Savor them. Take notes. Click on links. And most importantly, take action on what's appropriate to your situation and your business. Transformation won't happen without your action.

DR. MARYJO WAGNER

MaryJo shows heart-centered entrepreneurs how to move From Overwhelm to Inspired Action. Pick up her "35 Favorite Tips for Avoiding Distractions" at http://overwhelmtoaction.com Email her at maryjo@mjwagner.com

Table Of Contents

Introduction

Carla McNeil and Nilofer Safdar met each other during an online course in May 2010.

They started talking to each other via social media outside the course. They just had this connection between them and spent almost a year together where they did mastermind calls with each other, supporting each other through their business and that was really fun. There was always this idea to create an event together.

Nilofer had been creating tele-summits for about 3 years. She loved doing tele-summits, learned a lot and did a great job. Creating a tele-summit with together with Carla was a natural extension of that experience. Nilofer had been learning marketing, and really wanted to create a tele-summit on sales and marketing.

It was challenging to decide what they were going to do together because when they first met; through the online course we had very different areas of expertise and business models.

Carla was just starting to build a social media business and Nilofer was developing her business in healing, motivation, self-help and empowerment. In the beginning it appeared to be a real challenge to connect the dots between what they could do together.

The biggest obstacle was they actually live on the opposite sides of the world. Carla lives in Canada and Nilofer in the Middle East. What they both love about this is when you actually want to do something together, it doesn't matter what work you are doing, you can always marry the two together. That is the beauty of the online platform, one can be in Canada and the other in the Middle East and they can still create an event together.

Carla, with her social media marketing expertise wanted to make sure the experts delivered strategies and ideas, plans, different procedures the summit participants could use in order to market their business effectively. To be able to take advantage of all of the traffic that is available on the internet and to be able to put themselves in front of the people who are looking for them.

Nilofer, with her personal development expertise knew it was really important to get training and to have systems and processes and strategies in place to create your business, but she also knew that there was this other piece of the puzzle which is like the inner game. No matter how many courses you do or what you have learned in terms of marketing or in terms of strategies and things like that, you will not be able to get a lot of success from that if you don't have your inner game and what she means by the inner game or your mindset in place. We have all beliefs, mindsets around success, around making money. So even if you are putting in all hours of the day and you have done all the courses, but if you don't have the inner game in place, you will never be able to get the money, the success, the clients that you could.

As they worked together and supported each other, it became really obvious that the two needed to be married together in order for people to succeed, which is why the whole Best Client Summit was created around giving people the information from both areas.

They decided to create The Best Client Summit; the focus for each of the experts was; "What is the unique transformation you wanted to offer your audience?"

While creating the summit, the online event where they interviewed experts in the two different fields, Nilofer had the vision of having experts who knew the marketing piece, who knew the strategies and who would share the strategies, procedures, and systems for creating a business to be able to attract more clients and make more money. They also wanted to have the other experts in place, the ones who are experts in the inner game and who can help people in transforming their inner landscape so that they are able to have more success and attract more clients, more money and explode their business.

As the economy tanks or doesn't do well, especially here in North America, more and more people are searching for an answer online. There are so many different courses out there that say they are the latest and greatest and they very likely could be, but if you don't have that mindset in place going in the right direction, it's not going to happen. Finding and attracting your customers and clients online is quite different from a brick and mortar business. No matter what, we knew all the people who came to the Best Clients Summit, who participated are people who want to make a difference. You really can do that online, provided you have both your marketing and your mindset in place.

One of the experts they interviewed, Dana Garrison, said, you could be talking to ten different people all day long. However, if you have a belief system which says that, I can't have money and I am not good enough for this person, even though, you consciously may want to have that client, want to get their business, your belief system creates this energetic field around you which will have the client say, "No, I don't want to work with this person or I don't have the money", or, they will come up with all kinds of excuses. Whereas if you take care of the inner game, then what happens is you are exuding such an energetic field of attraction of charisma that the people whom you talk to will just say yes to whatever you are offering.

Their goal is for everyone to make the difference they want and build a business where they can treat people better than perhaps they were treated in their job. The other goal was to understand the difference between marketing and sales. In the beginning, many entrepreneurs don't quite understand the difference.

To make sure people understand the difference between marketing, which is getting the word out there and sales, which is actually talking to the people and bringing in the money, two very different things.

Basically, this book is a compilation of thirteen interviews that were conducted during the online event, some of them on the strategies, some of them on the mindset. When Carla and Nilofer were talking about the summit afterwards, they realized what the experts had shared was so valuable they just wanted to get this information to more people out there through a different media. And a book is an amazing medium to put your message out there. And that's how this book came about.

CHAPTER ONE

Business For The Future, The Changing World We Live In

BY GARY DOUGLAS
Founder, Access Consciousness®
Facilitator, Leader & Innovator
Author & Speaker on Consciousness

"Business for the future has to be a place where we see how we all contribute to each other and that we are all part of a greater good, and a greater possibility. Until that comes along, business as it currently is will always create upsets and disasters, and places where people are upset about things they don't need to be angry about. "
— Gary Douglas

For me business is another form of using your awareness to create something that's greater than what may exist. Most of us don't even know the way we should live our lives, we are creating our lives based on other people's points of views, and this is the way people create business too. It's very interesting to me to see that people don't actually look at everything that's going on in business. For example, right now, I see that there more and more store fronts that are empty. Everywhere I go, no matter what city it is around the world, there are more and more empty shops. That is just an indication of where the world is going. So much of our commerce has gone from small 'mom and pop' or local stores to international global networks and it's all network orientated more than anything else.

I think 'mom and pop' stores, also known as stores that are dedicated to selling one thing, or catering to one particular group of people, are on their way out. Right now the stores that you go into to look at stuff are the high-end stores. The people who have lots of money, still like to take their time to go and shop. The people having a tighter budget go online to find something, rather than using their time to shop. I know a lot of people that do 90% of their shopping now online. Is that just a passing fancy or is it a thing of the future?

We have to understand that we've gone through different cultural changes over the centuries. There was the hunter and gatherer, then there was the farmer, then there was the industrialist, and then there was the consumer, and now we have the Internet. These are major shifts economically, and major shifts in the way in which we do everything in our lives. We have got to be clear about what we're choosing and recognize that this is a time for us to look from a different place.

I've watched too many businesses and local stores go into business, then they're there for a year and after that they're pretty much gone. Why is that occurring?

Because what's going on is that the world is going to the Internet to determine what they're going to shop. They compare and contrast not by going to another store, but on what they actually have available to them at any one moment. So they will do a comparison shopping on the Internet. It means that they're going to look on the Internet, find their best deal and they're going to choose that.

People used to do a lot of trade, and slowly but surely the number of people that have the capacity to do those trades is going away. One of the things that I found interesting was when I bought an antique Automaton, a gadget that has a little man sitting on it that moves his hand and smokes his cigarette. I bought it in New Zealand and it was broken. The guy I bought it from said he would get it fixed before he sent it to me. So I bought it and when it came down to it, he finally said "I can't send this to you because I can't find anybody to fix it" and he really couldn't find anyone. Then he found a guy in California who could do it. I went to meet this man and it turns out that he's the last one of his kind doing this, and he can't get anybody to learn his trade. He fixes antique music boxes and antique Automatons and yet no one wants to learn what he does even though he's the last of his kind.

What are you going to have to create from when those things occur? Another example is the people that do upholstering. Years ago upholstery was something you did; you reupholstered your furniture. Now people go out and buy new furniture instead of reupholstering. The end result is that this area of upholstery work where people would upholster antiques is beginning to die out. The refinishing of antique furniture is dying out. There are a lot of things that have been the staple of the last hundred years that are disappearing. This is what's normal now in the scope of how the world functions and you have to be aware of these things or you're going to get caught in them.

Creating a Future

What is the future going to need? What would create for a future that would work for me? These are the questions you want to be functioning from if you're going to create for the future. As part of what I would like to create, I'm now looking to find people who can do these trades. Luckily there are still developing countries where they have people who learn how to do these things, and the great thing is they aren't that hard because I learned some of them on my own. You've got understand that there's a different possibility available for you and there is a difference between looking to create 'for the future' or 'in the future'. To create 'in the future', is when you go in the future and say, "I'll have one million dollars". In order to see that as a possibility you try to go into that future where you have one million dollars and work your way back to what's going to create your million. So you're working your way back to now.

You've got to create 'for the future', which is a whole other possibility. I create for the future based on, 'What am I going to need to know, what am I going to need to have, what's going to be possible now or in the future?' And finally, 'What would I like to create for the future?' It's just a difference then 'for the future' and 'in the future'. When you create 'for the future', you start today to build something that will come to fruition. When you start to process from 'in the future', you throw your future out and think that to get to your target, you have to work it back from where you have that money or that result and you work your way back to now and determine what you choose. Rather than going 'What do I choose today that's going to create the future I'd like to have?' One of the tools that I always give everybody is the question, 'If I choose this, what would my life be like in five years? If I don't choose this, what will my life be like in five years?' What happens when you ask that question is that you get to perceive the energy that choice will create for your future.

I want an expansive life. I'm not getting ready to retire; I'm not getting ready to die. I'm not getting ready to have a sedentary life, no thanks, somebody else can have that. So I'm looking to create now for a future that will be there when I get there. It's really important to do that. You've got to remember to ask, 'What my life will **be** like?' not 'What will it **look** like?'

This came up as a result of an experience: years ago I had friends that would work really hard for two weeks before their rent was due to get their rent together. As soon as they got their rent together, they would quit working. Then two weeks before their rent was due, they would start working really hard again to get the rent together. They were not creating for the future; they were not even creating in the future. They were living in the now to the best of their ability with the idea that, 'well I'll deal with that later'. None of those choices, dealing with it later, or dealing with it in the future, is really a good choice because you're not creating for a future where this is no longer an issue. So anything that you have as a current issue, think of that right now and ask yourself 'What could I create now that would allow for the future'?

Defining The Purpose Of Business

The first way I define the purpose of business is, will it be fun? I believe that you have to start creating for that future you'd like to have. When you get into a business, the first thing I'd ask is, 'If I create this what will my life be like in five years?' and 'If I don't create this what will my life be like in five years?' The other question I use is, 'If I create this, what will the world be like in 50 years, 100 years, and 500 years?' Why do I ask this? Because you have to guess that if the world is changing so fast, you've got to be prepared for seeing what's going to be in existence in 25 years, 50 years, 100 years, five hundred years. If we don't start creating for the future, the reality is that we're going to end up killing the planet. If you've decided you're going to do a business in pesticides, you can ask 'If I'm going to create this business in pesticides, what will the world be like in 50 years?' Notice the energy with that question, it doesn't feel very good. Now ask 'If I create this what will the world be like in 100 years?' that feels worse. And now ask, 'If I create this, what will the world be like in 500 years?' that feels even worse. That's because basically what you're doing is you're looking at the result of what your business will create, because every business creates something, so what do you want to create?

Money as the 'Result' of Business

Usually if you make money the purpose of the business all you think about is the money part of it. Therefore you must always cut costs and try to create more money and in doing so, you eliminate the creation that would actually fan the business and create more money. When you do it for money, you focus so much on money outflow and inflow that you forget the creative capacity of it. You've got to always look at business from what it will create. If you look at it from what it will create, a different possibility can show up.

Money is the result of having a business, not the purpose of a business. Most people start in a business because they have it as an idea to make money. You've got to look at what's valuable in other people's worlds to determine what you can do or be that will create that for you. Different possibilities occur under those situations. It's really important to recognise what you're shooting for here and what you're trying to create. If you start to look at what you're trying to create, you can look from a different place. You've got to have the possibility created by the questions, 'Will this business be fun, will I enjoy it, what will it create?' If you're looking at a business that will create something in the future, the reality is that you're creating it for the future. Ask yourself, 'If I create this, what will it be like in 50 years, 100 years, and 500 years?' When you ask these questions then you begin to see the advancement of where it will go, which means that it's going to grow exponentially. Why would it grow exponentially? It would grow exponentially because it's not only viable; it's truly a possibility for something that hasn't been. A business, in order for it to be a gangbuster thing, has to be something that hasn't been.

When they created personal computers, IBM went out of business because IBM didn't think that personal computers would be valuable. They did not see the truth of the future because they weren't willing to be in the question of 'what was'. You've got to constantly question to determine what might occur or what could occur if you're actually creating this business and truly creating it. That's why you don't want to focus on money. You want to focus on the creation of the business.

Ask every day, 'What can I be or do different today that will create more in my life right away, more money, more relationship, more business?'

Everything works in strange ways. I got involved with Costa Rican horses, I thought they were so wonderful. I thought the whole world was going to want them. So I started importing them and started breeding them here in the USA. It was a great idea, but right about the time I started, the horse market went down and disintegrated. Will the horse market ever come back? Probably, but not the way that I would like it to. The interesting part about it is that when I started looking into creating a place we wanted to create in Costa Rica, a resort, I realised, that if I have people come to that resort and ride these kind of horses, they're going to want these kind of horses, which means that everything I've been preparing for during the last five years will finally have a reason to be. I couldn't have got enough horses here in the USA to fulfil the need, and in five years I've created quite a herd of horses, which will give me a place to sell and have them available for people where they haven't been available before. It's a whole different level of possibility and it exists based on a choice that actually exists. People will go there, people will participate in the activities available, and that is going to create a different possibility for that business.

Another business I started was an antique business in Brisbane, Australia, where I got in sideways. Every week someone comes in and says "Wow! This is the best of the best! You have the best antique shop of any place I've been pretty much worldwide", which is quite amazing. But considering the fact that I buy most of this stuff because I travel around the world and send it over there, it kind of makes sense. You've got to get what you're creating and what it's going to be. Now, the Antique Guild has not made any money yet, it's still going in the hole, but I'm creating something for the future because in the future it will become so well known that people will be seeking it out to see what it has and what's available. I have bought things that I didn't even realise were as unique as they are because I just liked them. I thought they were pretty. I bought them based on that and the end result is that they ended up being worth a lot of money.

A whole different universe becomes available to us if we're willing to look at what's actually in the world. You have to look at what's intrinsically valuable to others before you do a business. You've got to see what it is you like about doing the business and if you do it because it's fun for you and you make it about expanding the possibilities with it, then the business will most likely grow, most likely succeed and most likely create a different possibility.

The Most Expansive Question To Ask

The question I would ask is, 'What am I not willing to perceive that I will receive here?' If you would perceive or receive that it would become clear because the only reason you can't get a feeling on it is because you've already decided something.

The next question to ask are, 'Where do I start? What do I do first?' A lot of people say that you've got to do your business plan so you can get money. What if you didn't have to get money or you didn't have to give a business plan? I always look at the business plan from the point of view of, if I want the money then I've got to have the business plan for the bank in the way that they want to see it. And who do I get to do it? I'm not going to do it because I know me. If I take all the steps to figure out what the business plan is, by the time I get the business plan done I'm never going to do it, because I've already worked out in my head how it's going to work in the first place, so I won't do it. Once you've figured out in your head how it's going to work, most of you will never do it. You've got to be in a place of a different possibility, and different choice.

The way to stop working it out in your head is by starting it. You just start doing it without going into the mentals of it. I have people that are always saying 'how are you going to do that?' I just ask if this is going to create the future that I'm looking for, yes or no? If I get a yes then I'll do it. Everybody goes, "Yes, but what do you do if it doesn't succeed?" My reply is "'If I don't succeed, maybe that's what it took for me to get to the future I really want to have." People think that the purpose of everything is to succeed. Well, sometimes failure is the beginning of success. Sometimes failure opens the door to what you really want to do. Sometimes failure gets you to different possibilities that you hadn't been able to see before. You've got to be willing to have that reality, not function from this strange thing which is, 'I've got to get it right first!'

How To Have People Show Up

The first thing you have to do is ask for the people to show up. I didn't start out that way. I had ten, twelve, and fifteen people in my classes when I began. I always kept creating and asking, 'What can I be or do different today to create more now and in the future?' I'm always looking for what's going to create more now and what's going to create more in the future. Why would I want more now and in the future? Because I'm not stupid, I know what I can do now and I know what's possible in the future may be two different plans.

Attracting The Right Business Opportunity

Ask, 'What would I like my future to be like? How much money would I like to have? How often would I like to work? What would I like to be doing?' What I did originally was I figured out that I wanted to be travelling a week out of every month, now I travel three to four weeks out of each month. I wanted to make sure that whatever I did was never boring because I get bored easily. I wanted to make sure that whatever I did or was would create a better world, improve the world in some way. Everybody asked "Well, what are you going to do?" I said "I have no idea", but I kept asking for that to show up. I would put that out in front of me, pull energy into it from all over the world, and if anything showed up that felt like that, I did it. It led me to what I'm doing. It's only because I was willing to have that place and space knowing that I could be led to it, if I could just acknowledge what it was that I was trying to create. Notice that in that I didn't say a single solitary thing about how I wanted to have the perfect life, I wasn't talking about the house I wanted or anything like that. I wasn't talking about anything else other than what do I want to do? If you look for what you wish to choose, something different will always show up. But you have no idea what it's going to take to create that.

Handling Overwork, Overload, and Overwhelm in Running your Own Business while Managing Time, Freedom, and Family Situations

Handling any of these things is not about you ignoring any of them, you just recognise the need to take care of them. You recognise what your priority is each day by asking, "What is my priority today?" I get up in the morning and I ask, "Where do I need to put my attention today?" This morning I realised that there was a piece of furniture that I had ordered and hadn't heard about in three weeks, so I knew I need to put my attention there. I realised that my front door was being worked on and I needed to check on that. I realised that I needed to check on some railings that I ordered that hadn't come in and they were supposed to come in over a week ago. So I started asking, "Where are these things? What's going on?" In other words, I put my attention on those. Then I asked myself, "Okay what else do I need to do today?" I know that by choosing certain things at the precise time it's going to create something greater in the future. It doesn't necessarily mean it's going to be greater for me, doesn't mean it's going to be greater for you, doesn't mean it's going to be greater for the world. The question I function from is, "If I create this what will the world be like in fifty years, a hundred years, and five hundred years?" Well, what I get is the world will be greater. How do I know that? Because the energy lightens as I ask the question. Now, do I know how that's going to occur? No, I haven't a clue, which doesn't matter. What matters is that I'm willing to do it, and be the question, and function from a different place where it's about creating more, not about having more. If you make your life about having more, what you end up doing is creating a place where nothing gets accomplished except the 'having more' which is not necessarily in your best interest. You've got to be willing to create more, and that will be in everybody's interest.

Carefulness with Money Shouldn't Limit What is Coming In

First of all I suggest you run a process, which is, '*What creation am I using to invoke and perpetrate the lack of generosity I am choosing?*' Then say the Access Clearing Statement™ to clear the energies that are creating the limitation in that area: *Right and Wrong, Good and Bad, POD, POC, ALL 9, Shorts, Boys & Beyonds.*

If you're careful with your money to too far a degree, you're actually being miserly and stingy with yourself. You've got to break that cycle. Then you've got to look at and ask yourself, "If I spend this, what will my life be like in five years and if I don't spend this what will my life be like in five years? If I pay this money what will my life be in five years and if I don't pay this money what will my life be in five years?" You'll start to see the expansion that comes from spending money and you may wonder, "How does that work?" That's not a question though, it's the assumption that there has to be a reason or a method by which it goes, which is not true. 'Does it work?' is not relevant. *That* it worked is relevant, and that it works is what you're going to be working with, not the 'how'. So you've got to get clear in this area if you're going to create a change. The question opens the door for you to choose to do these things; it's the only way you will ever create what you'd really like to now.

Stop Looking for the Right, Good, and Perfect Choice.

Realise that nothing is either right, nor is it good, or is it perfect. It just is. That's number one.

But number two, you want to run this process: *'What creation am I using to invoke and perpetrate the right, good, perfect, correct and best choice as the only choice I am choosing?' Everything that is will you destroy and uncreate it times godzillion? Right and Wrong, Good and Bad, POD, POC, ALL 9, Shorts, Boys & Beyonds.*

This process is really dynamic because if you're always trying to do the right, good, perfect, correct and best choice then what you're always trying to do is judge. You have to judge everything you do, everything you say, and everything that you are before anything can be created to really create what you want.

Ideally the process I would run is *'What stupidity am I using to create this stupidity I'm choosing in this area?' Everything that is will you destroy and uncreate it times godzillion? Right and Wrong, Good and Bad, POD, POC, ALL 9, Shorts, Boys & Beyonds.*

Because what happens is we get into this place of deciding that something should be a certain way rather than recognising what choices we have. You've got to look for the choice. If you're doing the right, good, perfect, correct and best choice, what you're really doing is looking for the judge-able choice.

What you want to do is run *'What stupidity am I using to limit and destroy the life changing, reality changing choices that I could be choosing am I choosing?' Everything that is will you destroy and uncreate it times godzillion? Right and Wrong, Good and Bad, POD, POC, ALL 9, Shorts, Boys & Beyonds.*

You start to get that you have multiple choice. You don't want to look for the little choices, which is, 'Which is the right choice?', those are always the little choices. You want the big choices, which is really about the bigger choice of 'What else is possible here, what else can be created here, what else would I like here, what would change my reality and everybody else's and what would create a different world?'

Q&A

I have two businesses; one is a cheesecake networking event business, and one is a coaching business. I find that my gourmet tasting events are fully booked and my other coaching events are no longer taking place due to lack of attendees."Am I to change it and give up my coaching? What do I do?"

Well, you know what I would do? I would go where the demand is. It doesn't mean that you give up one of the businesses, but it might mean temporarily that's where the attention goes, to the one that's successful. Perhaps people would rather eat than be coached. Feed their bodies and then eventually their soul will need feeding as well, so have the coaching available. Do what's creating the most money and the most possibility and the most choices and the most future. Just ask the question.

A question about the Access Consciousness classes:

"Not many people in my city seem to be interested in going beyond the Access Bars® classes. What question can I be to get even more people interested in Access and how do I get more people interested in going further in Access?"

Well for the time being, be grateful for those that come just for the Access Bars, and create as many Access Bars classes as you can because more and more people will come to that. Eventually there will be a few interested in more. When I first started the Bars classes about 20% of the people that did the Bars classes went on to Access Foundation or Level One. Of that 20%, only 40% went on to Levels Two & Three. You've got to get that there's a lot of people who want an experience or they're willing to do one thing but not necessarily another. They have a few judgments or a few thousand judgments about what they should do or can't do or have to do or ought to do or whatever. You can't expect everyone to do it and go on. What you do is find a few that do, be grateful for those and don't judge you or the others for what they don't do. That's the biggest mistake I see people making. They judge themselves or they judge the other for the fact that they don't go on to more. 80% of people will not ever go on. It's not a big deal. You've just got to be prepared for that and recognise that.

"I do Access Bars Classes and can't seem to create consistent clients or consistent Bars classes. I live in a small town and have facilitated lots of people there. I'm willing to travel. How can I expand the business? What question or clearing process would help?"

What energy space and consciousness can I be to have my business expand exponentially? Everything that doesn't allow that will you destroy and uncreate it times godzillion? Right and Wrong, Good and Bad, POD, POC, ALL 9, Shorts, Boys & Beyonds.

Keep running that thirty times a day and see what happens.

Judgments Just Shut Down the Whole Thing!

Yes, unfortunately most people don't get that. You're creating, you're creating, you're creating and then you go into judgment. The moment you go into judgment (and doubt is just another form of judgment), the moment you go into that, you shut down all the energy you started creating with.

The first thing is that if I feel any intensity of doubt, I ask myself "Who does this belong to?" Just ask this question every time you have doubt and if it feels lighter at all, then it's not yours. And after that, the only thing you have to do is return it to sender. What if you are way more psychic than you think, and you assume that all the thoughts, feelings and emotions you have are yours? Who's life are you living? You might consider that some thoughts, feelings and emotions you are having are not even yours. Doubt is never really yours. Doubt is something that you created as yours under the guise that this is what's necessary. What makes you think it's necessary? Is it really necessary or is there a different possibility that you haven't considered?

I suggest you keep running this in whatever energy space you've got, 'What can I be to create an exponentialising of my business right away?' Whatever your business is, it opens the door to a greater sense of everything that is actually possible.

"What if I have no idea what I want to do? I put the question out there what kind of contribution can I be to the universe? Nothing seems to come up to me that's obvious."

Those are not exactly the words you want to use. When you ask 'What would allow me to be a contribution to the universe?' it's actually just being you that creates that, so that's not really about getting what you'd like to do. If you're like most Humanoids, you do something for two weeks and you go 'I don't like this... I want to do something else.'

Humanoids are a different species of two-legged beings on this planet. They take a different approach. they are always looking at things and asking, "How can we change this? What will make this better? How can we outdo this?" They're the people who have created all the great art, all the great literature and all the great progress on the planet.

Humanoids only find out what they really want to do by doing things that they don't want to do. They go out and get a job and do something until they realise they don't want to do that and eventually what they'll do, is open the door to what they do want to do. It will come much easier than you think. But you want to go get a job and leave it, and get a job and leave it. Do you put that on your resume? No, you don't have to tell anybody that you worked there for two weeks and left. Do something that gives you a sense of what you're actually capable of.

Another thing I noticed is that most people are not willing to know how different they are and that they can do something that other people can't do. Why would that not be your choice? You've got to be willing to have that point of view. You've got to look at this and ask yourself, 'What would I like to do?' Do that energy pull tool that I said in the beginning. What would you like your life to be like? Do you want to travel? What do you want to do? How much money would you like to make? I started out with saying that I wanted $100,000 minimum. Now I'm up to $100 million because I decided what I was making wasn't enough even though it was enough compared to other people's universes.

Greatest Barriers in Business Growth

The greatest barrier I see is when you decide you have the answer finally. Especially the final answer because what you do with that is you keep looking for ways in which you can get it right. You think that if you get all the pieces in place then what is going to show up is exactly what you want. That's actually not the way it works. You have to be willing to look at a different possibility and ask, 'What would I really like this to be like, what would really work here, what's really appropriate for me?' Get the sense that there's a greater possibility in life if you're willing to have it. It's a slightly different point of view if you'd like to look at that. I would also recommend reading Steve and Chutisa Bowman's books, 'No More Business As Usual' and 'Prosperity Consciousness'. Those two books give you more insight into the mistakes people make because they talk about businesses that have made mistakes by not being on the creative edge of a different possibility. If you get those, you'll get the real pragmatic, down to earth, easy to use tools that create a different result.

"I share a business with my husband and I have my own business. My energies usually go towards my own healing business, which he puts down and criticises because it's not a moneymaker. How do I disregard his criticism and keep being joyful in both businesses and create more in both?"

Don't disregard his business. Put energy into his business so it works too. The one that brings you the most pleasure is the healing business but that doesn't mean it's the one that's supporting you. You have to put energy into the one that's supporting you as well as the one that you want to create. You're not a limited being, you're an infinite being. You can put energy into both businesses and ask him questions about his business and don't tell him anything about your business. Ask him, 'How was business today, how did everything go today, what was the best part of your day, what's happening, is there anything I can help you with?' Create the appearance of interest without the necessity of interest.

How to be on the Creative Edge in a Changing World.

You're going to be on the creative edge by willing to be in question; truly be in question. You have to look at everything that's going on around you and ask, 'What am I willing to be aware of, that if I was aware of it would create a different possibility here, a different choice, and a different reality?' Those are the things that will give you the awareness that you're looking for. What you want in a business is always a constant state of an ever-increasing awareness, you can ask, 'What energy, space and consciousness can my body and I be that would allow us to have an ever-increasing awareness?'

Why Don't We Choose?

Well, all I have to say is that there is a lot more out there available that we could choose if we would. We don't choose because we keep thinking, "Well, I'm doing this business so therefore I've got to keep going." One thing about you as a humanoid, is that you really need five to ten things going on at all times in your life. If you had five to ten different things going on in your life, a whole different universe would open up for you. What would it take for you to have that, allow that, or be that in some different way? So you've got to be looking at it and ask yourself, 'Okay, so what can I actually create or generate here that I haven't considered, what is really possible that I don't know about, what else can I have, what else can I create, what else...., what else...., what else?' And the most important thing that I see people doing is, rather than seeing the gift that they are and functioning from that, they keep trying to get it right. Thinking that if they can get it right then things will happen. No, things will always happen but what you've got to do is instead of being willing to 'get it right' you've got to be willing to 'get in a conscious state and create in a constant state of possibilities.' When you get that, everything becomes a choice; everything becomes a place where people can create from. It's amazing how few people bother to create. That's really when I ask the question, 'What can I be or do different today that would create this right away?' If you function from that then greater sources show up. That's how I've created every business I have and I have eight of them.

Looking at Business as a Distractor Implant

There are people that when they look at things from a business point of view, it's all about how much money they're going to make and what they need to control and how they need to control it. This shows up when you function from business as a Distractor Implant, in other words, when business is not a creation but a distraction from what you can create and generate in your life as well as the world. Recognizing this, and using these tools is about getting you out of that place where you're the effect of what you think you need so that you can move into the creative possibilities. Creating your business is really the most important thing, and that comes from being the question and choosing.

Deal and Deliver

The deal and deliver is where you get very specific about how you create every sort of contractual agreement you have. You become very clear about what people will and will not deliver, and how and why you end up with problems. There is a telecall that I did on this topic, and that call came about as a result of something that Dr. Dain Heer, my business partner, was doing. He had what he thought was an agreement with a lady, where she said she would do a job for approximately this amount of money. In the telecall I say, "Number one, when someone says 'approximate' say I'm sorry, I will not deal with approximate. Exactly what do you want?" Then the lady asked if she could have a class Dain was doing as part of her deal? He said yes. The original cost was *supposed* to be about $2,400. He gave a class, which was $1,200. And she sent him a bill of $4,500. He was horrified and asked, "How can you charge this?" He didn't understand how she could do this. I said to him, "It's really easy. You never made it a confrontation of exactly what it's going to look like, and exactly what it is she was going to charge" He never got her to say that. Dain was then trying to defend his point of view and she had already made her point of view, so neither one of them can change any time. If you're going to create deals with people you've got to get out of that defence. The thing about the deal and deliver is that it takes you out of the place where you're defending a point of view or trying to get a point of view across. You're actually willing to see what's possible and start creating more. It's one of the best things with business that I've ever seen in my life. It's always the way I've done business but I sort of didn't recognise it.

The 'What If...' Series.

Oh yes, now we're talking! What if everything was possible and nothing was a problem? What if your choice created everything? What would create a different universe? I'd like to acknowledge that people who have used these tools have found that they were able to get everything they really wanted. As a result, they were able to have more than they ever thought was possible. That's really from my perspective, that's what business should be. A place where you get to have whatever you want and whatever you choose as a greater possibility and not a lesser one.

The Access Consciousness Clearing Statement

The Clearing Statement is a tool you can use to change the energy of the points of view that have you locked into unchanging situations. You are the only one who can unlock the points of view that have you trapped.

Clearing Statement: Right and wrong, good and bad, POD and POC, all nine, shorts, boys and beyonds.

Right and wrong, good and bad is shorthand for: What's right, good, perfect and correct about this? What's wrong, mean, vicious, terrible, bad, and awful about this? What have you decided is right and wrong, good and bad?

POD is the point of destruction immediately preceding whatever you decided.

POC is the point of creation of thoughts, feelings and emotions immediately preceding whatever you decided.

Sometimes instead of saying, "use the clearing statement," we just say, "POD and POC it."

All nine stands for nine layers of crap that we're taking out. You know that somewhere in those nine layers, there's got to be a pony because you couldn't put that much crap in one place without having a pony in there. It's crap you're generating yourself.

Shorts is the short version of: What's meaningful about this? What's meaningless about this? What's the punishment for this? What's the reward for this?

Boys stands for nucleated spheres. Have you ever seen one of those kid's bubble pipes? Blow here and you create a mass of bubbles? You pop one and it fills in, and you pop another one and it fills in. They're like that. You can never seem to get them all to pop.

Beyonds are feelings or sensations you get that stop your heart, stop your breath, or stop your willingness to look at possibilities.

It's like when your business is in the red and you get another final notice and you go argh! You weren't expecting that right now. That's a beyond.

(The majority of information about the clearing statement is from the website www.theclearingstatement.com)

COOL INTERVIEWS!

To listen to all the interviews that created this book, including the interview with Gary Douglas, visit http://crackingtheclientattractioncode.com

---

CHAPTER TWO

Business Owners Stand out from the Competition - Be The Celebrity in Your Field

BY CRAIG DUSWALT

Creator of the RockStar System For Success – How to Achieve Rockstar Status in Your Industry
Rock Star Marketing
Green Room Design & Advertising
Axl Rose's Personal Manager touring with Guns N' Roses
Air Supply Band's Personal Assistant

"Being a one of a kind means we are automatically the best in the world at what we do."

— Victor WIlliamson

The journey from being the personal assistant for Guns n Roses & Air Supply to the personal manager for Axel Rose to starting my own marketing rock star business has been incredible. Before I did all that Guns and Roses stuff and Air Supply stuff I was a marketing major in college and did some marketing before I left. So I did have a marketing background. I also had an acting background. That's how I had some stuff before I actually went on tour for eleven years. The transition was easy when I got back out of the Guns and Roses World because I just wanted to be normal again and I did not want to be on the crazy whirlwind of a tour.

When I got home from a tour I said I'm just going to settle down and go back to the roots which was marketing. I got a job as a proof reader right away and then I went from proof reader to copywriter to senior copywriter within three months, and six months into the company, I became their creative director. I went up very, very fast because I had a great background and I did a lot of work with those bands and I think they liked that.

So I got back into the world of copywriting and the marketing and the creative director. Then I went to a Tony Robbins seminar and everything changed and I decided I wanted to become an entrepreneur. I didn't want to work for anyone anymore because at the advertising agency where I was working at as a creative director I was doing all the work, but they would get all the pay cheques. So instead of letting them get the pay cheques, I just got the pay cheques and I opened up my own advertising agency, Green Room Design and Advertising. My clients included Baskin Robbins, the Los Angeles Dodgers, ESPN and the Academy Awards. I had some pretty big clients.

I became a speaker through a total fluke and that's where I am today. I basically speak all over the country on rock star marketing. I teach regular business people how to become known as rock stars in their industry. I don't teach people to sing, I don't teach people to play guitar, I just teach them how to think outside the box and do things differently than everyone else does and to think like a rock star. Most importantly believing in oneself like rock stars do. There are a million things that rock stars do that I learned touring with Guns and Roses and Air Supply that we as businesses should do as well to stand out from the competition and become known as an expert and celebrity in our field. That's what I do now and it all stems from going to college for marketing and years later I'm finally using my marketing degree.

Marketing-Guns n Roses Style

I have a story and I am not saying this really happened, just saying it to put things into perspective. We'd be in Denver Colorado and we'd have a concert and then the next show was in Kansas City for example. Denver was sold out but Kansas City had Arrowhead Stadium which seats eighty thousand, but there's only forty thousand people coming to the show. The show is in two days and we're thinking about how we're going to get forty thousand more people to come. Someone might have said... " oh let's throw a television out the hotel window." And someone would do that, maybe. (They'd make sure no one was below us obviously so no one got hurt) Then the press would come and they'd say "Oh my God Axel Rose has been a bad boy again, Guns and Roses is acting up again... What are they going to do next in Kansas City when they come? We'd be in the press, and we'd make sure we got into the press. I'd call the local newspaper and say ... "I think I just saw Axel Rose throw a television out of the hotel room, you might want to come here." We'd set that all up.

So the next day the tickets would go crazy and Kansas City would be like... Oh Oh what's Axel Rose going to do next? And we'd get in the newspaper. Now I teach businesses how to do that, how to get into the media, how to get some press releases out, what can you put in a press release that will attract them to whatever they want, how to talk about something that gets you in the news on TV and on radio. That's basically rock star marketing, it's getting in the press and doing things differently than everyone else so they want your story instead of someone else's.

The Unique Transformation

The unique transformation is to just think differently. For example real estate agents send out postcards with their picture on it and a little sold sign and say I can sell your house. Well, you've got to do things differently, this what every real estate agent is doing.

I teach people how to write a book, I teach people how to get on radio, why they should get on radio, why they should have their own radio show. I have a jewellery store owner that used to be one of my clients. I told him you need to write a book, he was surprised, and said "why would I write a book about owning a jewellery store?" I told him it would teach people how to buy diamonds. It would explain the whole rating system of a diamond, its colours, the flaws that you look for etc. And the light bulb went off, now no other jewellery store owner is writing a book about their business except for this guy and now he gets more people. All of a sudden you're the expert and celebrity in your field because you've written a book. Any business can write a book, real estate agents, loan officers, gym owners. Any business at all can write a book about their business and their system of how they do things and teach people how to use their system. In this way you create a client base. There's something unique in everyone's background, something different about every single person otherwise we'd all be the same person. So when I coach people I always say... give me some of your background. We talk about their background and what they have done differently.

When I first started, I was America's Shoestring Budget Coach, and I was teaching people how to save a ton of money on marketing and advertising. I knew how to help people save a lot of money because I used to charge $10,000 to design a flyer at my big advertising agency and now you can get them designed for $25 at Elance.com, Guru.com or similar sites. I thought alright I'm going to save the world a ton of money on marketing and advertising because I know how people can get this stuff cheaper than going to a graphic designer or an ad agency. I did that, but the transformation came when I went to a mastermind group. Though everyone liked my idea of being 'America's Shoestring Budget Coach,' they said "but you have this incredible background in music industry, why aren't you using that?" And I said to myself, oh yes, I don't know, I'm the marketing expert, but I couldn't see what was right in front of me. Right in front of my face was this opportunity to use my great background with Guns & Roses and Air Supply and just incorporate that into my brand.

I was at a mastermind... they told me to do this... I went upstairs and I came up with the 'Rock Star System for Success- how to achieve rock star status in your industry.' And everyone in the room was clapping, they said "that's it, that's perfect!" I still teach the same exact thing. I teach people how to save a ton of money on marketing and advertising, but now I just use a little rock star twist to it. Teaching people to think different and my whole career has gone through the roof. Just because of the one little switch I made in my brand. One little unique transformation, I put the word rock star in front of marketing because that was my background.

I had this thing and I believe everyone has something. People say to me " You toured with Guns and Roses, that's a cool background and of course you're going to use that, but I don't have that, I didn't tour with Guns and Roses, so what do I do?" I tell people this little thing all the time. There's a company called Fiscar Scissors, they make scissors and I'd never heard of them before I did some research on line, and found that they're like the standard for the scissor market for people who do scrap booking. They even have a community called Fiscarteers. If a boring thing like scissors can be this major thing where they have a community of tens of thousands of people that talk about their Fiscars scissors on line on social networking then you have to have something in your background that people have in common with you. And that's what you pull out when you're branding yourself. So the unique transformation is basically finding something different in your background, thinking differently and obviously believing in your-self that you are good at what you do. If you don't believe that you don't have the right mind-set, then all the marketing I teach just goes out the window.

Something Different/ Unique

There's something different and/or unique in everybody. I coach tons of people but for the first hour all I do is talk to them. When I coach them, I ask them to tell me something about their life. One client is a real estate agent and she hates real estate but she's good at it. She loves baseball, so now she calls everything 'the home run' or 'the stolen base' and things like that. She's incorporated baseball into her brand of real estate and now she loves real estate again.

Maurice De Mino teaches people how to put together their presentations. He's Italian. So we came up with 'the Sicilian Men-tor' and anything that he does is about the family and the pasta dinners at his seminars. All he did was take his ethnicity and put something in his brand and now he's The Sicilian mentor and he teaches people how to kill from the stage, meaning how to do great on the stage. There's always something there, and we didn't even have to go that far back. We didn't even have to find something unique. The unique thing was he's an Italian and he spoke like this and mama mia everything and it was great. He wasn't the total Italian guy that we're thinking in our heads right now, but he had enough of it. Now in his seminars he is, and he turns into that. He took what he already had a base of and pushed it to the next level.

The first question I always ask people is... who is your target audience? When they say well everyone would like my stuff, I either run the wrong way or I hit them. You can't have everyone as your audience, it just doesn't work. I mean I would love to say everyone is my audience because I'm a great speaker and everyone should listen to me. But as soon as I do that I've watered down the brand and there's no focus. You have to choose one thing. Most people don't do that. They try to do too much they try to cover too many bases. But if you just focus on one niche, one audience, then that's how you become successful.

I tell people sooner or later your brand will find you. But you've got to throw it out there. Most people are afraid to release something because they're not sure if it's perfect yet. And if it's perfect then you're too late, because it is going to take you years to become perfect. Just like my shoestring budget thing, I wrote four books on shoestring budget. I wrote Marketing Your Business on a Shoestring Budget, Creating Wealth on a Shoestring Budget. After writing a series of books on Shoestring Budget, all of a sudden I'm into rock star marketing. I switched everything after writing four books and printing two thousand copies of four books. Normally I'd say oh my gosh, what did I do? What a waste of money. But it's not a waste of money because if I didn't throw that out there then someone wouldn't have come to me and said why are you not incorporating music in your brand.

I always tell people that you've got to throw something out there. Do something and if it's the wrong brand the right brand will find you. Then when they find you when its correct then make sure you stick with it. Brands take time to develop, and most people will do something and two months later they'll say okay that's not working, move on to the next and then two months later that's not working move onto the next. And that's daft. You just can't do that. You have to stick with something eventually. You know you've got to stick with something and you get enough feedback that by throwing yourself out there that sooner or later you're going to have to trust a business coach or a mastermind team. That's why I believe in masterminds so much. Because there's a group of people out there that is willing to help. I have a hundred and thirty people in my mastermind and we have a private Facebook page, everyone puts up an idea and we all say yes that's a good idea, what about this? And within a month everyone has a pretty solid brand because they get a hundred and thirty different opinions. That's why masterminds are so important and that's where I found my rock star stuff. Most people aren't focused and they try to do too many things and it gets very messy.

Attracting Clients

Let's say I have a seminar coming up in March. I already have three hundred and sixty people that have paid and are coming and I want five hundred plus. My goal is to have six hundred people but I'll just say more than five hundred people. I need about a hundred and seventy more people, plus the cancellations at the last minute. So I want at least a hundred and eighty more people. There are about a hundred and seventy days between now and that boot camp in March. I need to get one sign up a day and that gives me a hundred and seventy more people and puts me at five hundred and thirty which is a nice number. I know I'm going to get more people because I guest speak all over and I sell 20, 40 to 50 to people every time I do guest speaking. So I'll be way over that number. All you have to do is get one person a day, one paying person a day and you do not leave the phone or your social networking or whatever to get that one person, until you get that one person. You get that one person and then you're done for the day in that aspect of your business. Say I got a person today at 7:35 AM and its now 12:20 PM, so five hours ago I got my one person. But I'm focused on getting 5 more today because it was so easy to get the 1st person. I always tell people if you can get one new client a day whether they buy your book, CD, workbook or your system, one person a day and you're going to be so much better off.

But on top of that what I'm really good at is how I attract clients. I'm really good at doing forty different things to get ten people, instead of going with the attitude, 'I need to get four hundred people' because this overwhelming. I try to take the overwhelm out of everything. So I have forty different ways of getting ten people. And some of those include chat rooms. I do guest speaking. When I guest speak I always sell my products and my rock star marketing boot camp. That's why I teach people how to become a professional speaker, and you need to speak on your subject so that you can get hired or asked to speak at chamber events or local associations or local networking groups and just upsell whatever you're selling. Usually it should be some sort of seminar even if you're not a professional speaker. Then I teach people how to write a book, and as soon as you write a book, game over you win, because something changes. I have this client who wrote a book on how to have a stress free mortgage. She's a mortgage broker, a loan officer. As soon as she wrote that book, her client base went from forty clients a year to a hundred and forty a year. We think it's a direct correlation to the book, because if I'm going to choose between two mortgage brokers, I'm going to choose the one that hands me a book instead of the one that hands me a business card. So I teach people to write books.

Then there's radio. I have a rock star radio network. It's an internet radio company. We have sixty regular business people that have radio shows. And it is amazing the credibility that you get in this world when you tell someone that you have a radio show. They don't understand the difference between internet radio and regular terrestrial radio, they just know you have a radio show.

The perception is you must be really good at what you do if you have a radio show.

I go into chat rooms and I discuss things that have to do with my boot camp. For example I toured with Guns and Roses, so I talk about Guns and Roses and that I used to be Axel's personal manager. I tell them the stories. Then they always say what are you doing now and I say I'm a motivational speaker and I teach rock star marketing. And they go oh my gosh, I have a company I need rock star marketing and then they sign up for my seminars. We have a conversation about Guns and Roses which has nothing to do about marketing but eventually it turns to "what do you do now?" I tell them I teach marketing and they usually need marketing because they are probably working for a company or they have their own company or they want to make money on the side so you get people. You go in chat rooms of like minded people. A lot of people love photography, so you go to chat rooms about photography. A lot of people love cooking so you go to chat rooms about cooking. Golf, go to chat rooms about golf. These are major keywords that are used in search engine optimisation (SEO) because people love photography, golf, recipes and those things. So you go to these chat rooms and the conversation eventually turns to 'so what do you do now?' Since you've formed a relationship with this person, you say I put on these seminars or I do this, or I provide this service, or I'm a coach or I'm an author, I just wrote a book. And they want to buy it because you're like minded and you have something else in common instead of just going after the sale all the time.

I go to Guns n Roses and Air Supply chat rooms, those are my obvious ones. But then I also go to Kansas City Chief chat rooms. I'm a huge Kansas City Chief's football fan so I go to those chat rooms and we talk about the Chiefs and football. It's just back and forth football, football, football. Eventually the conversation gets going and then I say I put on these marketing boot camps every March and September in Los Angeles. I'd love to meet you in person and you can go sign up for it right now online. People sign up left and right.

Keywords are the Key

Key words are good for search engine optimisation (SEO). If you can somehow tie in golf, or recipes, or grey hair into anything that you do then you can get more hits. And I teach people how to do that at my boot camps, to use these keywords that have really nothing to do with your business. You can come up with a blog or a story or a Facebook post that incorporates those words into what you're talking about. For example if I go play golf I'll say... Oh on the golf course today I was thinking about this, this, and this and it reminded me of marketing tip. So use the word golf, or golf tip, or golf course or golf whatever and then tweak it to a marketing tip. I got tons for hits because people were Googling that and I now have ways of getting them to go to my blog using those keywords that are very trendy. I teach people how to use trends on Google and YouTube.

What Not to Do

Even though I made a mistake with Americas Shoestring Budget Coach, I didn't really do it wrong because I still threw myself out there, and I was still getting speaking gigs, but I just made it better.

What people do wrong is after a while they become indifferent. A lot of people think I'll build the website and I'll do this internet marketing thing and not have to leave my house and I'll just do that and then hopefully it will just start selling things because I put it out there and hopefully people will buy it. But you need to get involved, you need to go to events, you need to have your own events, you need to get on the radio, you need to write a book, you need to get out there and that's why I teach rock star marketing, because as crazy as rock stars are, they're all great marketers. The ones that make it in business are great marketers. All these bands that play locally at New York City, Los Angeles, Chicago, Miami and Detroit are good. But the ones that know how to market themselves are the ones that stand out. They do the social networking and they have people that do that for them but they also do it. And they get out there they do concerts; they show up!

Another thing that doesn't work is not showing up, two seminars ago we had six hundred and twenty four people registered, they actually paid money and I think four hundred and eighty showed up. It boggles my mind that a hundred and forty people paid money for something and said at the last second you know what I just can't make it. I just don't get that especially if they're in a business and they paid for something and they want to learn. I understand some things happen that prevent them from coming but that's rare. I had a lady who said I cannot make your boot camp because the only time I can get my dog groomed is that weekend. I almost fell down, I was like you've got to be kidding me!

The other thing that doesn't work is the whole focus thing. You know they try to do too much and that's what doesn't work. Oh I will give you something that doesn't work, I just remembered. It did work but I did it differently. A lot of people said you know you're teaching me all this marketing and that's great but I don't even know how to start a business. So I thought to myself okay I will teach them marketing but I will also teach them how to become an entrepreneur. So back in March, I switched the name to Rock Star Entrepreneur Conference. And it went great and everyone was happy. But for me it was too much. I was teaching how to raise money, how to start a corporation, how to run a business, how to hire employees, and then marketing on top of that. Well I was doing five day seminars before that on marketing alone. And now they're down to three day seminars and then I added how to be an entrepreneur on top if it and for me it was just too much.

I don't know if the people felt the same way but for me it was just too much, too much, too much. I learned that I needed to go back to my roots. So my boot camp was back to Rock Star Marketing Boot camp.

Not that it didn't work, the Rock Star Entrepreneur Conference, but it didn't work for me. Because I said that's just too much, I'm teaching too much and I'm not really getting into the core of marketing. I was kind of just glossing over marketing instead of just really getting deep into the marketing. Things like going into the secrets of YouTube and how to get a lot more hits on YouTube that I couldn't do because I was teaching too much.

There's a lesson right here. Just focus on your area of expertise and don't try to grow too big, just go deeper into your brand. And that's what I've done now. I went back to Rock Star Marketing Boot Camps and teach more marketing instead of just glossing over the marketing. I go really deep into the marketing and people love it. And I loved it because I was able to do what I do best which is marketing.

Everyone tries to do too much. They say I've done this for a little while, I want to do something else and that's the kiss of death in this industry. In any business just do what you're good at and spin it in a way that makes it fun for you because if you don't love doing it then you're not going to succeed. You have to love what you're doing, you have to have a passion for what you're doing, and if you've been doing it for ten years and you starting to get bored on it then switch it up, but still teach the same thing. You already have this base, don't try to figure something new out when it's working. If it's already working stick with it and just tweak it a little.

Books vs Visiting Cards

I teach rock star marketing, but I wrote four books in nine weeks, so everyone wanted to know how I wrote four books in nine weeks. Now I teach Rock Star Book Writing, how to write a book in thirty days and how to self-publish it. By doing that people can say well now you're teaching book writing and I say no, I'm teaching people marketing, because I believe in marketing. One of the best ways to market yourself or your business is to write a book. So I just went deeper into my brand instead of trying to come up with something new.

Imagine it, you're at a networking event and there are two people that do the same exact thing. One of them hands you a business card which is what everyone does and the second person standing right next to him hands you a book. I'm going to do business with the person that handed me a book because anyone that can write a book...is very organised their thoughts, is an expert in their field and must have done something really good to get all those words to form a book. So in my mind that person stands out right there. The other thing about handing out books at networking events instead of handing out business cards is as soon as you hand out one book to one person then another person comes over and says, "what are you doing?" and I say "oh I'm just giving out my new book would you like a book, it's called the Rock Star System for Success." I give out those books for free when I do networking events and I hand out a couple of books and then I get ten or fifteen people surrounding me because they all want a book.

Most people ask why it is called Rock Star System for Success? I say well I used to tour with Guns and Roses, I was Axel's manager and now I teach regular business people how to become rock stars in their industry. Then they want to know more about Guns and Roses because that just opens the door for conversation. Then I give my website out and that night half of them go home and sign up for my boot camp.

It just helps me stand out from everyone else that just gives out business cards and to tell you the truth, if you listen to what I teach and how to write a book in thirty days and how to self-publish it you can print them for about a dollar a book. And yes it's a little bit more than business cards, don't get me wrong, but the bang for the buck is so much better with the book. If you order two thousand books for about a dollar a book then you're paying $2,000, if you sell two hundred of those books for $10 each you got your $2,000 back and you have eighteen hundred free books left over that you can hand out for free, and that's the way I look at it. I use my books as a business card not as an income maker. Now I make money at it, but that's not the attitude that I have. This is my business card and basically here's everything about the rock star system if you like it then sign up for my boot camp.

I teach people to write ninety six page books and they're not hard cover they're soft cover. It's a perfect bound book, they're called perfect bound books, you don't want a stapled book, you want the spine on the book. A ninety six page book takes the 'over-whelm' away, you don't have to write a three hundred page book. My first book that I was going to write six or seven years ago was a big marketing book, almost three hundred, four hundred page marketing book. Everything you need to know about marketing was in it and it was going to be like the bible of marketing what-ever it was. And then I went to a seminar and this guy holds up a small book, like a sixty four page four inch by four inch book and he goes here's my new book. It looks like a coaster it doesn't even look like a book. That's when the idea struck. I had this big idea for a book and in six years I had written just twenty pages because it was overwhelming. So I took each chapter of the book and turned them into their own book. Each book now is ninety six pages and it's very un-overwhelming.

People think that they only have to write ninety six pages they end up writing a hundred and twenty, a hundred and fifty page books anyway. But the attitude going in is I only have to write ninety six pages there's like five pages in the front and five pages in the back where there's no writing on it at all, so I only have to write eighty six pages and then the chapter, that's one whole empty page right there. And if I have ten chapters then I only have to write seventy six pages and then the 'overwhelm' is totally taken away. They say "I can do that" and then they write a book, they get their name on a book and their picture on a book and it changes everything. I wrote four books from the one book I would have written. I was going to write a lot more but then I switched to rock star marketing. I get way more credit for writing four books than I do for writing one big book. I'd rather be an author of five books than one big book, and that's the attitude that we have going in.

Rock Star Entrepreneur

The rock star entrepreneur is basically a person that has gone through my course and is now able to think differently. I have about sixty or seventy outside the box marketing ideas, just wacky things you can do too. I teach people to run for their local office because you get to put those signs everywhere around town and you get name recognition. I teach these outside the box marketing things that people can do and by doing that they just become rock star entrepreneurs because they start thinking differently about marketing their businesses differently. Then it becomes an attitude because I believe in my heart that I have a passion for what I'm doing and that I'm good at what I'm doing and for whatever product or service I'm offering is worth way more than I'm charging. If you can get that attitude and the right mind set and add some marketing secrets or marketing tricks or marketing tools to the mix then you are a rock star entrepreneur.

HAVING FUN YET?

YOU WILL when you sign up for the interviews! To get more tips, strategies and ideas that can help you integrate your business and create the success mindsets to attract a FLOOD of your Ideal Clients, grow your business and make 1000s of $$$$$$

Visit http://crackingtheclientattractioncode.com

CHAPTER THREE

Sacred Sales Conversations and Converting with Consciousness

By Amethyst Wyldfyre

Chief Excitement Officer, Amethyst Wyldfyre Enterprises, LLC
Empress of Empowerment, International Speaker
Multiple Award Winning Entrepreneur, one of America's Premier Experts
Author, Award Winning Recording Artist, World Class Wealth Healer

"Each of us is a unique strand in the intricate web of life and here to make a contribution."

— Deepak Chopra

I've been selling in one way or another for most of my life. It started when I was a child and sold Girl Scout Cookies – the year I was 9 – I sold 763 boxes of cookies – over 30 times as many boxes as the next highest seller who sold around 20 or so boxes. I now specialize in helping people who have an important, powerful, inspirational, motivational or life changing message to not only be heard by millions but also to be able to make millions in sharing that message too.

Often people are "called" into serving and following their spiritual path but they don't really have a good grasp of the selling conversation and how vital it is to their service to the world. There are two main problems that I see that can come up for people in this – one is the problem of not being in a good relationship with money yourself (as the messenger) and two is not really knowing how to or being able to powerfully show up in the "asking for money" conversation – which has three main challenges of it's own that I'll explore later.

First Let's Look At Your Money Relationship

When you have issues yourself with money, and that doesn't mean that you're not making money, it doesn't mean that you're destitute or in poverty. Like many of my clients, you might have issues around money in the following areas:

- Receiving money
- Holding/Growing money
- Channelling money through your personal life or your business
- How the government participates in our money system
- Taxes
- Spending money
- Investing money
- Saving Money

- Redistributing Money
- Charging/Using Credit

If you have issues in any (or all of) these areas, then having the selling or conversion conversations with other people to invite them into work with you will automatically set up circumstances where your own money stuff is going to be put right in your face. For example, if you have issues with credit cards, then it's likely that one or more of the people that you're talking to about coming into your work, will have something come up with the credit card – like when it's time to seal the deal they can't find it, or the card expires part way through your service delivery and you have to chase after them to get the new number, or it simply won't process no matter how many times you attempt to put it through.

If you have issues around paying taxes or you have issues where you can only allow yourself to have so much and not any more, then when you get into these sales conversations, you're bringing your energy field to the conversation. You're bringing your stuff to the conversation just as much as the person on the other side of the conversation is bringing their stuff.

It's incumbent upon anyone who wants to be of service to do two things. First of all, they have to consciously choose to actively build, grow, enhance, and enjoy their own personal and professional relationship with money. Secondly, they must be able to have these selling conversations because if you're not selling, you're not serving and you don't have a business, you have a hobby.

The Beginning

My life path has been real interesting. I used to be in the real estate industry and I was in a partnership with two men. The men had no issues with money apparently, but I did have issues with money because I ended up in a situation at the end of that career where

I was on the short end of the stick in terms of how much money was flowing my way. It really had nothing to do with the partners. It had to do with my own stuff around money. On the outside it appeared like I was very successful. On the outside it appeared that I was making a lot of money and to me at the time it seemed like a lot of money. I had a lot of judgments of myself. I had a lot of thoughts that... 'well I didn't have a college education when I first went into that business and into that industry, I didn't have a ton of experience and I was a woman and young. All of these thoughts kept me in that small space. It was very interesting because it was like there was two of me. There was the outward me and there was the inward me. The outward me looked very successful. I was building and developing a multimillion-dollar community with two partners. It was an award winning community. I became the national chairperson of my trade association. But the inner me was feeling completely like a caterpillar inside the cocoon, which is basically mush. The inner me was like mush and had no clarity around my own value and worth.

Then I had a spiritual awakening and that spiritual awakening completely got me out of that old business and into higher levels of consciousness and into my own personal healing, and ultimately eventually led to me becoming a mentor to people who I'm serving around the world now that are messengers. People that have a world changing or field-changing message for their field of expertise and are really seeking support in finding their own authentic voice, sharing their message with the maximum amount of people that they possibly can reach, claiming their true value in the marketplace and monetizing that message.

The evolution of my journey is that in under 3 years I created a multi-six figure business in my pyjamas from home, speaking virtually, and serving people around the world to raise their consciousness to become more empowered personally and professionally and to bring their big messages that are meant to be served into the world that need to hear them. My business has now generated over 7 figures (over $1 million) in total revenues and continues to grow.

Selling Yourself & Your Work - The top three challenges when it comes to Asking for Money:

The first challenge that I see people face when it comes to asking for money is the challenge of the "over-giver". This is when someone is really serving their gifts into the world and not getting money in return, or not getting enough money in return for the results they are helping people to achieve. I'm going to illustrate this with a little story about my own journey. After I left the real estate business and became a healer, I discovered that I was really gifted at healing and had no idea. It was something that was completely not on my radar screen up until that point. I discovered that I was very gifted with the healing capacities that I had been given including the capacity to see into the soul at a very, very deep level. I had no context for how to price my work. I had no context for how to serve my work into the world. Most importantly, I had a framework as a woman, and I think it's a woman thing although I have seen it happen with men as well, there's more conditioning on the women around over giving.

What happened on my own journey was I actually started my own art gallery and healing arts centre. I funded the building and creation of this from my proceeds as a real estate developer. For two years, I promoted thirty one artists and I had all these other healers in my space and I was promoting them. I was doing my own healing work as well. Financially it did not add up correctly. I was putting way more in financially than I was getting out. Eventually after two years, it became very clear to me that I had to stop or I was going to end up with no money at all. I had a child to feed and mortgage to pay and my own needs to be met. I had to stop doing what I was doing. What I find a lot of healers especially and also women mentors, and coaches, and trainers do is they just give, give, give, give, give and fail to value what they've been given as gifts in a monetary way. That is the number one challenge, the challenge of the over-giver.

The second challenge I see is the challenge around being attractive and pursued, and it's really interesting because you wouldn't think this would be a challenge but I've seen it happen for a lot of people. What this means is you have this beautiful gift, you have so much to offer to the world, and yet you want to hide because there's some fear of being seen, of being heard, of actually being attractive and pursued. When you are in business, it's so much easier, so much more energy efficient if you allow yourself to be attractive and pursued rather than having to go after clients or go out there and hunt down business. When you are attractive and pursued your clients naturally want to work with you whereas when you're out hunting down clients, it's almost like they come into the relationship disempowered.

For me, it's super important for my clients to actively seek to create the change because then energetically there's already momentum. Many people really are hiding. They go into coaching programs, mentorships, start doing things like branding and getting their website set up and doing all of these things but they're not ever having a sales conversation. They're never putting themselves out into a space that says 'I have something to offer, I invite you to come and have a conversation with me about this'. It's easier to be working 'on your business' than working 'in your business' because working in your business means you have to be attractive and you have to allow yourself to be pursued.

Challenge number three is the challenge of mastering power in the form of people's energy coming into your business and the money that comes into your business. I had one client. She first made a huge leap when she stopped over giving and she allowed herself to become attractive and pursued. Suddenly she went from a six figure business to a seven figure business. When she came to work with me the work was all around helping her to step into her power and her leadership role so that she could actually manage, contain and hold the money that was now coming to her and the people and the clients that were now coming for her. She needed to be able to hold energetically the space to allow all that to come in.

It's kind of like the story of the people who win the lottery. They'll win a million dollars, or two million dollars, or a hundred million dollars and the next year it's all gone. The reason why it's all gone is because they don't have the capacity to manage and master power in that way and hold power in that way. So that is the third challenge that I see happening with people in the area of having these sales conversations and allowing themselves to manage and master people's energy and the energy of money that is coming through their business. This basically represents the energy that the people are investing to have a transformation happen for them.

They receive the money but they can't hold onto it or build anything with it. You need to be able to actually hold money in order to build the infrastructure of your business and to be able to delegate tasks that you shouldn't be doing. For example if you're an extraordinary healer what you should be doing is your extraordinary healing and you should have somebody else doing your bookkeeping. You should have somebody else doing your client intake. You should have somebody else helping you figure out what you're doing for your marketing. Your role as the extraordinary healer is to transition as quickly as possible into just doing your genius. There are steps along the way that sometimes you actually have to be doing more things 'in' your business than you're supposed to be doing. But the fastest way for you to build a business is allowing yourself to shine your brightest light and to have sales conversations and bring in money, because the money allows you to delegate and get the support that you need.

The Sales Conversation – Come Out of Your Shell So You Can Sell!

I use the acronym **SHELL**. This is my formula for having powerful sales conversations and conscious sales conversations. I want to step back before I give you the formula and talk about these conscious sales conversations because when you go into a sales conversation thinking... 'oh I need to make my next payment on my mortgage and I've got to get a client right away', your consciousness level is really in scarcity. It's not in abundance, it's not in wealth, it's in a place of scarcity. When you come to that conversation, you're holding that energy. I do understand that sometimes you have to go through your own shift around being in scarcity with money first, which is one of the things I said in the very beginning. You've got to have a clear relationship with money yourself in order to really potently be able to put these principles to work and it's a process. Not to worry if you feel like you're somewhat in scarcity, this is for people that are there. It's also for people who in abundance. It's mostly for people who really want to shift to a place where they are creating consciously a container so their work lives on for an extended period of time and does a lot of wonderful things in the world.

The container, the formula that I have for having a sales conversation begins with you as the purveyor of what you are selling. You are the person that is selling a good, a product, or a service. You've got to start the conversation by standing your ground and owning your own greatness. If you're in, and this is for people who are on the edge of scarcity where they're like... 'I'm just starting out my business or I'm trying to put my business together and I haven't figured out this sales conversation piece yet, I'm feeling really nervous and I'm a little bit in that scarcity mode, then how you shift to be able to stand your ground and own your greatness in your journey is by remembering that what you have to offer has nothing to do with where you're at financially. What you have to offer is a gift from spirit and is your unique gift. If you can start by valuing that then it takes any money issues you might have out of the equation.

I definitely recommend that people get clear with their own money relationship first. However I understand that there are people in process. Just having the awareness if you have a scarcity mentality, just me shining the light on it right now is enough for you to be able to make a choice to step into getting support for yourself around your own money clarity. So standing your ground and owning your greatness is the first step in the money conversation. You've got to be able to be so confident in what you have to offer and also appreciative. That's another beautiful way to help you shift. When you can appreciate and be in gratitude for your own gift, then you will be able to be more grounded in that gift and more confident in presenting it as an offer.

A lot times people think that they might be gifted, but they aren't sure that they're gifted. I want you all to start from the place of knowing that these gifts come through you, that you were uniquely born to deliver whatever it is that you deliver and that if you weren't called to deliver this gift, you wouldn't be equipped for it. The first step is learning how to have that faith in yourself and if you can't have faith in yourself, then have faith in your Spirit. Your Spirit will always hold you as long as you maintain that connection. That's the first step in the formula. Stand your ground and own your greatness and the greatness that's coming through you.

The second step in the sales formula conversation is **H** - holding the space for the person who is coming to you in struggle. One of the reasons why I'm talking a little bit about the people in scarcity is because I want them to know that I can hold the space for them and I can recognise that they're in that story, but I can also say to them that you can come out of that story. I can hold the space for them to see that they can step out of that story into a new experience. An experience of abundance, an abundance of money, an abundance of clients, or even an experience of wealth, which is where your business is actually working for you and you're overflowing with so much money that you're at total choice about how you spend your time. You're at total choice about how the money gets channelled and you have built a support system around you that is funded by the money that comes through the business because the business has taken on a life of its own.

So when you're at the selling conversation, you want to hold the space compassionately for your potential client. Regardless of where they're at on the spectrum, say... 'I get where you're at and I'm holding this space for you to step out of where you're at into a new space'. That goes back to the S – stand your ground and own your greatness. You are in the position as the person who is making the offer to support and help this person; you're in the position of being on the other side of the fence from their story. It's your responsibility to hold the space that... 'I have all the compassion in the world for anybody's story and they have a choice, they can either step into the space where I'm going to help them, facilitate for them, assist them in empowering themselves to get out of their story, or they can go off and not exchange money with me and keep their story'.

That's cool! You (or your prospective client) can keep your story if you want. My job is just to hold the space that it's possible to transform and transmute this story. This is a story that happens all the time when you're selling. When you're in a selling conversation somebody will say to you... 'well I really think that I need to do this work with you, I really want to do this work with you, but'.... And usually the "but" is I don't know how I'm going to pay for it or I can't see my way clear to making that level of an investment, or whatever they've decided to tell themselves for a story.

When we get to that point where you're feeling energetically that there's a "but" going on there, the next step is **E** - educate the prospective client on the results that they can achieve by making this investment. As you are educating you are making the connection for them that is connecting them to what they have already said that they want. If somebody comes in to have a conversation with you, the first thing you need to do is really get clear on what is it they want. What are their expectations?

We want to educate and we want to get clear on the expectations. If their expectations are for something that you can't possibly deliver, then you shouldn't be making an offer and at that point the conversation needs to end. It's no longer a sales conversation because it's become clear that they're expecting something that you don't have the capacity to deliver.

This **E** part of the conversation is really important. It is a conversation. You're exploring, you're educating, and you're getting clear on expectations. If somebody wants to work with you and they want to lose four hundred pounds, but you specialise in just losing the last ten pounds, then they need to go to somebody else to lose the first four hundred pounds.

When we're in the body of the conversation, we're doing a lot of exploration. We're getting clear on expectations and we're educating about what's possible from working with us and results matter.

I'll use my own business as an example. I was just on the phone with one of my clients who went through my Money, Magic, and Clarity course last Spring and generated $8,000 in money miracles within days of finishing the course. Since then she has completely changed her business model as a result of doing that course. I talked to her the other day she said... 'money is pouring in', just literally pouring into her new business model because she took that clarity course. Results matter! She had $8,000 in money miracles almost immediately and since then has had multi-thousands of dollars come into her business after making a shift in her business model.

When you're in the education part, when you're sharing what you can offer with somebody, make it clear that not only is there a process behind which that can happen, but results happen when people 'do this work'. I have had my own results from doing my own Money Clarity course. I have had many other people who I have taken through the process who have had amazing results including people that have had 300% increase in their revenues as a result of getting clear with their relationship with money. The E step is the meat of the sales conversation. This is also the step where you are evaluating whether or not the prospective client is going to be amazing, fun and empowering for YOU to work with – you want to be choosing your clients not chasing them.

Step four to coming out of your SHELL so you can sell is **L** - for Love! Love yourself, love your stuff, and love your prospect. The way you love yourself is by being willing to ask for money for what you offer. If you are out there doing great work and you're not getting compensated for it and you're not having sales conversations and you're not feeding your own coffers, then you're out of alignment with love. You've got to love yourself and you want to be giving from a place of overflow not a place of being empty. Love yourself enough to ask for money. Love your stuff meaning whatever it is you're offering, whether it's a home study course, or a group coaching program, or a mastermind, or private work with somebody, no matter what it is, love what you're offering. Because if you don't love what you're offering and you're just selling it to sell it rather than because you love it, people can feel that. That's going to cause a challenge in your ability to generate revenue. I went through a period of time where I stopped loving what I had to offer. When I stopped loving it, I had to stop offering it and I had to go back to the drawing board and offer something new. Finally, you've got to love your prospect. This goes back to what I said when you're holding faith. That is if they decide that they want to keep their story, then you've got to love them enough to let them go. If they decide they want to move forward with you, you want to love them enough to open your arms and say... 'welcome, welcome! I'm so excited to start working with you'! Regardless of the decision, love your prospect.

The final **L** is... 'Let go and let God'. This step is about surrendering the entire process up to Spirit, to the Great Spirit. The people who are meant to be your clients will always arrive exactly on time fully capable of investing in themselves and your work as long as you're not attached to any particular outcome. When somebody does say yes to themselves and to working with you, you want to be 100% committed to supporting them to get the results they are seeking. You want to be committed, but not attached. You want to be committed to this sales process but not attached to it either. That means that you have to get into the rhythm of having regular sales conversations knowing that you're going to be rejected multiple times and remembering that even the best people are not chosen every time.

It's so important to be clear on the fit, like I said before about the four hundred pounds versus the ten pounds weight loss specialists. If your specialty is helping people get that last ten pounds off then you really have no business helping the person wanting to lose four hundred pounds. Somebody else is built for that. These sales conversations are actually opportunities to weed through who's a fit and who's not a fit. The ones who are not a fit, it's not a rejection of you and it's not a rejection of your gift, but you're going to have plenty of those conversations. That's why it's super important to also have your own network of referral partners so that when you do have a conversation with somebody, if they can be better served by someone else you can refer them. Now you've done a service no matter what. You've done a service for some-body in the sales conversation no matter what.

It's Not Only About The Money

The number one reason to have conversion conversations, aside from the money piece and aside from building your own business and feeding your own business, is remembering that people are there to make the choice to invest in themselves at no matter what level. They do this by putting money, time and energy into what-ever it is that they are investing in, to help them move their own dream forward. Whether it's training, coaching, home studies, programs, products, services, by making that commitment to in-vest in themselves they are making a commitment to their calling and they're making a commitment to the people that they are here to serve. When you don't open the door for that, when you stay in a place of fear around asking for money, then you have not only closed the door to your own success and the potential for working with great clients but you also closed the door to all of the people that your clients could impact and serve and the door to your own gift too.

Be Willing... Not Judgemental

The people that appear to be the most desperate can actually cre-ate the most incredible results. It's like the four hundred pound person. When somebody loses four hundred pounds everybody's like... 'holy cow, look what happened to that person! What a huge investment it took to lose that four hundred pounds'.

When people make a choice to say yes to themselves and yes to their calling; the Universe conspires on their behalf, the Uni-verse starts to line up on their behalf. I have seen the most unlikely people come to me. I had one woman who had money that she had stored in her mattress, she said... "I'm receiving welfare" and she was really in a struggle. She had money stored in her mattress that she pulled out to invest in herself in one of my programs many years ago. I'll tell you it was a big step for me to hold the space for her to take the last of her available cash to invest in herself through my work. Big, big, big. I had to get over feeling sorry for people. When you feel sorry for people, you're buying their story.

I have another client story that I'm going to share with you and it goes back to what we said ... 'if you don't open the space to have the sales conversation, not only are you shutting off your own gifts you are also shutting off the potential for your clients and all the people they serve. I had a woman at one point who came to me and she had a vision. She was awakened and had a vision to create a space for people who were sitting with friends or loved ones who were dying. She was a photographer with her own photography business and all of a sudden she had a spiritual awakening and in the spiritual awakening, this group of beings came to her that she calls her mother guides and the mother guides wanted her to serve by creating a special place of support for people who were sitting with dying loved ones. She was shocked to have a spiritual awakening. That's the first thing that happened to her. The second thing that happened to her was that she felt totally inadequate to be able to do this.

When I intersected with her, it was almost immediately after she had her spiritual awakening. So the Spirit put me in her path right after her spiritual awakening. I was able to affirm for her. I said... 'yes, you absolutely had this experience, yes you are absolutely hearing from a higher level of consciousness and yes this is your task to do'. Her response was... "this is way too big for me, I could never be good enough to be the person to bring this out into the world". I ended up in a sales conversation with her, and brought her into my work. At the time my work was called the Core Path to Clarity. This was several years ago and my work has evolved since then to new and deeper levels. I brought her into my work that I was offering at that time. Literally within six weeks of finishing our work together, Stacy had written a book called The Soul Sitters, had launched a site soulsitters.com and now she has an international platform where she's serving people who are soul sitters and has created a foundation to support this work and keep it out in the world.

Just imagine what the cost would have been to the world if she allowed her feelings of inadequacy to prevent her from doing this work. Imagine what the cost would have been to the world if I had not stepped in and had a sales conversation with her to bring her into the work that I did with her that allowed her to overcome all of her feelings of not good enough, not big enough, not equipped enough to be able to bring this work out into the world. And imagine what the cost would have been to all of those soul sitters who are now supporting their dying loved ones as they make their passage.

Here For a Transformation

In every acorn is an oak tree, but the acorn doesn't know that it's an oak tree. What I'm going to say to those of you who are having those thoughts of well what I have to offer isn't that big. What I will say to you is regardless of what your judgment is around what you have to offer, what you have to offer must be offered. You must begin to exercise your asking for money muscle. You must begin to get yourself out there and start selling because you have no idea what an instrument for spirit you are until you start to sell and as a result of selling, serving. When you are in that service, miracles happen that you aren't even aware of. Parts of yourself that you don't even know exist become activated and you just may discover that you have a hell of a lot more to offer than you ever thought you did.

Say you knit baby clothes. Get out there and sell those baby clothes. Not just knitting the baby clothes, but it's selling the baby clothes. You just have no idea the goodness that can come from putting your gifts out there into the world. Those baby clothes could end up on the queen's new grandson, or great grandson, those baby clothes could end up warming a starving homeless child somewhere. Those baby clothes have in them your love and your energy and the gifts that you're here to give. Knitting the baby clothes and hiding them in the closet and not putting them out there is not going to do anybody any service.

I think a lot of people stay in their small space because they have a fear of money and they're not clear in their relationship with money and they don't recognise that money is something that's sacred. I love helping people to get started on the path of working with their message and with their money; those are the two areas where I mostly serve my people.

My main focus is to help people who have a message, to get that message out into the world. But I discovered as I evolved and grew, the money piece is a huge hindrance for a lot of people that was really preventing them from serving in the highest and best way possible. I also love helping people to get clear in this relationship with money.

I believe that we can always, always, always, no matter where we are on the spectrum, whether we're already serving people, we're already doing those sales conversations, we're already working with clients and we want to take ourselves to the next level or we're just at the beginning and we are fumbling around and don't even know where we're going with our business or we're in a place where we are starting to think about how we're going to accumulate wealth so we can leave a legacy, we need to have that support with the money relationship being clear. No matter where you are on that journey with money, you can always improve your relationship again and again and again and again. In improving your own relationship with money, it will allow you to hold the space for people in a sales conversation so that they too can step into their own greatness.

Get Help & Give Others the Opportunity to Get Help from You

All of the gifts that we have come through us, they come from our source through us to be served into the world.   90% of the success in making a shift is just showing up. I created almost a half a million dollars in under three years. I'm now over a million dollars in revenue. And how did I do that? I created all this revenue in my pyjamas by doing two things.

Number one, when I needed help with something whether it was my own money stuff or learning how to sell or getting clear on my message or improving my relationship with my son or my relationship with my Spirit, I asked for help from my upstairs team. I prayed to my Spirit and said... "I need help with this", and I was given an inspiration and I took inspired action and I invested with mentors myself.

Number two, how did I create half a million dollars in under three years in my pyjamas speaking around the world virtually? Because when I was speaking virtually, I was having selling conversations. Let me repeat that....I was having selling conversations. I delivered a lot of great content and I made an offer at the end for people to buy in order to make an investment in themselves. I was having private selling conversations as a result of those people coming into my community and getting to know me better and deciding they wanted to work with me. I gave them a way to get on the phone with me to have a private selling conversation. The two main keys to my success, half a million dollars under three years in my pyjamas and now over a million in total revenues generated speaking and selling from home – Getting Help for myself and Giving Others the Opportunity to Get Help from me through having the conscious conversation that converts prospects into clients.

Take inspired action, tune into your spirit, ask for help, offer your greatness and be willing to receive. It's like every time I'm willing to receive more, magically and miraculously more arrives. I'm super grateful and very, very, very excited to see where we go from here! What is next for all of us because it gets better every day! Our brightest futures are being activated now.

LOOK AT YOUR MONEY RELATIONSHIP

Listen to the interview with Amethyst Wyldfyre as you consciously choose to actively build, grow, enhance, and enjoy their own personal and professional relationship with money
http://crackingtheclientattractioncode.com

CHAPTER FOUR

Expand Your Message, Make A Bigger Difference, And Make More Money

By PJ Van Hulle
Founder of Real Prosperity, Inc.
Creator List A Palooza
List-Building Rockstars

"Definition of Insanity - Doing the same thing over and over again and expecting different results."

— *Albert Einstein*

The first major turning point for me came when I was living and teaching in Japan. I taught there for two years and knew that it was time to come back to the United States, that my experience was complete even though I was so happy. I still dream about Japan, it was awesome but I knew that it was complete and it was time to move on. When I thought about coming back to the United States I felt depressed because I had had it beaten into me from the public school system that you need to build your resume and get a job with good benefits. So I was envisioning myself finding a job and commuting for the next forty years and I was thinking okay, well the fun is over and I wasn't looking forward to coming back to the United States even though I wanted to see my family.

Around that time I happened to stumble upon this luxurious purple book in one of the bookstores and it was funny because where I lived there weren't very many books in English. Usually you had to go to the store in Tokyo. This book just grabbed my attention and it was 'Rich Dad, Poor Dad' by Robert Kiyosaki and it talks about the things that rich people teach their children and poor, middle class people don't. For some reason, I felt compelled to buy this book which was very out of character for me because I wouldn't normally buy a book that I'd never heard of and at Tokyo prices. But I did buy the book and paid $40 or $50 dollars for it.

I read it and then all of a sudden everything transformed, I learned about passive income, I learned about building business-es, I learned about investing. I learned that there were other ways than what I had been taught and had drilled into me. All of a sudden this entrepreneurial spirit that I had as a small child was re-awakened and got permission to come back out.

When I was little I was doing all sorts of entrepreneurial things, I would make cupcakes and sell them to my mum's friends and clients, I would run little contests for other kids at my school. I was always doing these little entrepreneurial projects but some-how this spirit got squashed down by the, 'you've got to get good grades, you've got to build your resume, and you've got to get a job'. So now that spirit reawakened and I realized that there's a place for me. I was so inspired and even a little angry because I thought..., why don't people know this? Why aren't we taught there's an alternative to just having a job until you're 65 and then retiring? Why are no other options presented to us?

I remember thinking people needed to know this. That was the big thought and from then on every time I'd go to Tokyo I'd not miss a chance to go to the English bookstore. I would get as many books as I could carry on real estate, investing, network marketing, sales, accounting, the stock market.... anything related to the things I was learning from the book Rich Dad, Poor Dad. I would just come home with two big bags. All the books I could carry every few weeks and then I would just devour them. I distilled all that into one simple decision, which was, I want to learn how to build businesses and invest and create passive income and live life on my own terms from a place of freedom and a place of joy. I want to teach other people how to do it too because if I'm depressed by the whole 'work 9 to 5, till you're 65' idea, there's probably other people that this model doesn't work for either. I want to show them there is another way because it was really powerful for me. So that was the first turning point.

The second turning point was I got really clear on how I wanted to do this...I wanted to become a speaker, lead seminars, create informational products and write books to get this message across but I had no clue how to do it.

I'm the kind of person that jumps off the cliff and develops my wings on the way down. I thought that seminar leaders lead seminars. So I put together a little seminar and invited everybody that I knew, and it was $10 for a 90 minute seminar for everything I knew that I didn't see taught anywhere in my area. It was about prosperity, consciousness and financial education. I had nine people come, so I made $90 at my first seminar. I was absolutely thrilled in every cell of my body because I felt that I was living and doing what I was put on this earth to do. I thought if I died tomorrow, who knows what the ripple effect and impact in the world would be for me sharing this with these nine people. It was enough money to pay for the hotel room that I had rented in Leha, Utah, and then I rented a karaoke machine later that night and had fun singing with people. It was great, it was one of the best days of my life but I didn't know where to go from there. I thought, well that was great but how many of these little $90 dollar seminars can I do?

Then I went to a workshop that was 'marketing and sales for holistic practitioners' and I wasn't a holistic practitioner but I figured that with my winning smile they wouldn't turn me away. So I went and they said "we teach people how to lead lucrative life changing workshops and we teach people how to create informational products and books and get your message out there in a bigger way." I was like... oh my God! That's exactly what I want to do. I felt like the universe or God for it just opened this door that I didn't even know was there.

It was really scary, I had left my credit cards at home on purpose, saying okay I'm not signing up for anything but it was exactly what I wanted! Their program was way more than I had ever invested in an educational program before so it was definitely outside my comfort zone. But this is what I'd been asking for, it was now presented to me, I wouldn't say no to that. I took their workshop and their program. The next workshop I delivered was a two-day workshop. I made $52,000 in one weekend, which was a big difference from the $90. That was how I got started in the seminar industry and quickly had a six-figure business doing something that I really loved. I felt I was really making a difference in the world and I've been doing that for seven years now. I've been able to make anywhere from one hundred something to three quarters of a million dollars a year in sales.

The third turning point was getting more into internet marketing because I was doing all live events and it was getting kind of tiring. I was thinking this is it?... I want to be able to impact more people and I want to have more ease and flow in my business. The reason I got into the seminar business was that I wanted more freedom for myself and other people and I was not experiencing that. I don't remember what the exact click over was but one part of it was definitely meeting my friend Micah Mitchell. We met at a workshop and formed a Mastermind group together. He was doing a seminar in Costa Rica on Marketing On A Mission and how to use the Infusionsoft program. I said to myself... I've had Infusionsoft for ten months and I still don't know how it works. I feel like I'm just throwing money down the toilet, so let me go learn. When I learned what it could do and what was possible I was amazed.

I dove into Internet Marketing and started getting clients and sales from people all over the world. Having lived in Spain and Japan and travelling to many different countries, I've always loved having that international feeling. Being able to take my company from a local California based business to having clients and strategic alliances and friends all over the world, really feeds something inside of me.

Doing Things Differently

One of things I do very differently than most people is instead of just saying I can't do something I ask myself 'how can I do it'. I keep learning; I'm a lifelong learner. Even now with all I have accomplished over the last fourteen years, teaching and seminars and learning all the new strategies and programs and actually doing it, I still go to seminars and hire coaches and mentors all the time.

I think part of it is having the learners' mind-set, the growth mind-set because growth is one of my highest values. I think the other part is anytime I was confronted with *Wow this feels really big or this feels like a stretch*, instead of saying to myself I can't do it, I thought "How can I?" This happens all the time, when I signed up for my first seminar, when I bought my first house. Initially it always feels impossible but I believe that there are at least ten solutions to every problem.

I remember I signed up for a $50,000 Mastermind and I had just $1000 to my name and no credit and I thought... well I have four days to come up with $50,000. This is what I feel is the next step for me how am I going to do it? I came up with as many solutions as possible however crazy. I told my inner critic that she could go take a coffee break. Mathematically I broke up the $ 50000 and decided I could sell 50,000 things for a dollar, or I could sell one thing for $50,000. I could sell off some assets that I have, I could maybe sell part of this program to somebody else, or maybe I could find somebody to sponsor me, or lend me money.

So I just went through all these things and eventually about four of those options came together and worked. This process is something that I've used again and again to help me stretch beyond what I might think is possible for me.

The Zing Clunk Test

To find things that work for me I need to have that feeling inside. Then I do something called the Zing Clunk test. It is just asking myself is this a zing or a clunk for me. A zing is like my body goes zzzzzz like this is the right thing, it feels exciting; I can actually feel a zingy sensation in my body. A clunk is like uhhh, it's heavy and it does not feel good. I don't base all my decisions just on that but the point that I want to bring up here is that if something is feeling completely in alignment, resonating, zinging and calling me forward, I feel that's my inner guidance system saying yes! This where you're supposed to be even if you don't know what it looks like or how it's going to happen. If you have that zinging feeling and then you go into "how can I do this?", I think that it usually works. If it comes from some other place like greed, lust or do I really want to do this because it's a good deal even though it's not necessarily the right thing for my business and me then it doesn't work the same way. So check in with yourself and find if you feel you're being called here or not.

The Transformation

The strategy I'm focusing on right now is helping people build a large profitable email lists. The reason I'm focusing on that particular tangible result is because one of my highest values is freedom and I feel that it is one of the easiest, most risk free ways to expand your message, make a bigger difference, make more money, have more ease and freedom and joy in your life.

The reason I'm focusing on building a profitable email list with people is again it comes back to that decision I made back when I was in Japan. I really want people to have enough flow and passive income in their lives so that they can make choice from a place of freedom and joy instead of debt and obligation and really live life on their own terms.

I have a special place in my heart for women entrepreneurs in their fifties and sixties who don't have enough money to retire by traditional financial planning means. But I serve lots of clients, lots of age ranges, men and women but those are the people that are a sweet spot for me. They're really special to me. I feel the traditional financial planning doesn't offer a viable solution for them. They're faced with having to work forever and God forbid if something happened where they couldn't work or they didn't want to work so hard they would just be screwed basically. I feel like the traditional financial planners don't have the answers but actually building their list and building up their marketing and sales online can actually make a difference.

I have a real estate background. I had thirty-five properties all over the United States. I got wiped out by the real estate crash and went from being almost able to retire with $6,000,000 in real estate to being millions dollars in debt and going bankrupt within a matter of months which was very traumatizing as you can imagine.

But one of the things that did for me is now I know what's involved in getting a piece of real estate to give you a positive cash flow. If you wanted to find a piece of real estate that gave you a $100 a month positive cash flow after all the expenses, i.e. paying the property manager, repairs and utilities, etc. There's a lot involved to that, I mean it's a lot of searching, finding and verifying information to find the right deal. Then if the numbers do work and it is actually a good deal you have this intense maintenance energy of managing the managers. Even if you do have help, a lot of unexpected things can happen. Like I've had people steal the copper pipes out of my buildings. I never could have predicted that. There are creative things you can do to do no money down but more often than not there is down payment and closing costs and other expenses.

When you compare what it takes to get a piece of real estate to give you that cash flow versus what it takes to generate $100 a month online automated, the online strategy is so much easier and less risky, less liability. It's way better and that's why I'm focusing on that because I feel like it's the easiest, least risky way to create more passive income and more ease of income. Even if you're serving clients and it's not totally passive it's still easier if you have a list of people that already like you.

Know Your Clients

One thing that really helps is knowing who are your ideal clients, who do you have that special place in your heart for because once you know that then you can speak directly to them. Understand their wants, fears and desires and speak their language. When you can "speak their language" to them it really helps your marketing. You can more easily figure out where they congregate so you can show up. You have your marketing showing up where they already are getting together. You can decide who else serves this group and make strategic alliances, joint venture partnerships and cross-promotional relationships with other people who serve the same group.

For example one of my top strategic alliances is Thrive Academy they teach people 'heart selling conversations.' It's basically sales conversations that come from the heart versus hard selling. They work with practitioners, speakers, coaches and consultants, there's a big crossover in the people we work with because I too work with practitioners, speakers, coaches and consultants which means a lot of our people are the same people. They're teaching them one on one conversation sales skills among others. They're also my mentors who taught me the seminar business and how to create info products. Most of my clients need that training too, so I refer to them all the time. However they do not offer programs on building, nurturing and monetizing the list, so when people go into my programs then they can learn more about marketing on a mission and how to attract clients and sales online.

It works very nicely because we're serving the same group of people but we're serving them in different yet complementary ways. These things make a big difference. When you know who to target you can even start doing paid advertising. It's something I've been doing in the last couple of years and that's worked really well for me.

Marketing on Facebook both free as well as paid advertising allows you to show your ads exactly to the type of people who are your ideal clients. A lot of effective marketing and sales comes from knowing exactly who those people are. This can be a very gremliney conversation because a lot of people I work with can help lots of other people, so it's hard to really take that stand and say this is the group that I'm working with. One way to get yourself out of that trap of being scared to pick or scared to commit is to instead of marrying a niche or target market you can first try dating it. Just like you would date a person before you decide you want to marry them. You can date a niche market by creating a tele-summit for them and you do one event that just targets this particular topic. You can also create a special free report or a tele-seminar just for them so you don't have to rebrand your entire business and make this fancy website, get business cards and everything. You can do just one little project for that niche and see how you like it, how it works for you.

For example, I've been doing a lot of work around prosperity consciousness and client attraction online for a long time. When I decided to List-a-Palooza, my ninety-day list building challenge it didn't fit exactly in with what I was doing with my business. It felt like a little bit of a tangent but I was so passionate about it, I had such a zing around it, I wanted to do it and I didn't care if it did not make any money. It was something that I was passionate about and I wanted people to have it. I did not know what was going to happen but believed it was going to be awesome. What happened was it did make a lot of money and I did have over 5,400 (fifty four hundred) people all around the world participating in the first one and about 7,000 (seven thousand this year. I actually became like a little mini celebrity, everywhere I go whether it's Whole Foods or seminars or whatever people are like you are PJ Van Hulle I'm on your list, I was on List-a-Palooza. Seriously, everywhere! People will stop me in the grocery store, I'm like wow, how did this happen? Once again I think that when you follow that zing and that passion and feel like this is what I'm supposed to do even if I don't totally understand why, I think that you're kind of being guided and nudged in that direction.

Now I'm going deeper into the list building world and started creating more programs around list building and we'll see where it ends up. I really love this and I just want to talk about list building, which is how I'm feeling right now, if I still feel that way next year then I'm going to entirely rebrand. People are already calling me the queen of list building. Most people make up their titles, like 'I'm the millionaire maker'; they made that up yet people didn't call them that. But in this case people just started calling me The Queen Of List Building, wow if multiple people are calling me this maybe there's something there.

Getting the Clients to say Yes

People are charge hundreds of dollars for the upgrades for their telesummits. The first one I charged $97 but I've seen people charge up to $500 to get the recordings, transcripts, worksheets, etc., the whole package. One of the things I feel very strongly about with List-a-Palooza is that I really want people to have this in their research library even if they're not going to listen to every single call. Also I don't want to have to go through the hassle of putting up the recording and taking it down and putting it up and taking it down, I want people to get it and have it easy and be affordable. During my tele-summit I made my upgrade only $27. A lot of people would say I'm way undercharging and I kind of agree because for the information and the value that's in the kit. If I was going to be selling that from stage I feel I could easily sell it for $500. I didn't want their money issues to get in the way, $97 you have to think about it, $47 you still have to think about it a little but at $27 there is practically no resistance. Why would you not do that, it's one night of Thai food maybe. I actually made way more charging $27 than I had made charging $97. I didn't know that was going to happen but the one thing that helped was really looking at what's going to make this easy for my clients and what feels in alignment for me.

If you can have somebody invest even $1 with you, it really shifts the relationship dramatically because now it's not just somebody that trusted you with their name and email address, they trusted you with their credit card information, address and phone number, it's a much larger show of trust. Start a potential client with a small investment right away and they're more likely to buy later, it's a deeper relationship.

What I started doing was not only making this insane ridiculous offer but making it immediately, as soon as people sign up for List-a-Palooza the next page says, hey, congratulations you signed up here's an insane offer for you that I think you're going to like. It gives them the opportunity right there to invest in the $27 kit. I felt nervous about doing that because some people say you shouldn't make any offers to your list for ninety days, give them a chance to get to know you and nurture the relationship. Making an offer too soon is too pushy. My experience is when I shifted to taking them to a sales page right away my sales quadrupled, just from that one little shift instead of waiting.

Also you want to deepen the relationship right away, and one of the ways you can do that is to have them buy something. One thing I did that I haven't really seen before is I created something that I call an initial sales letter. It's a typical sales letter, with the days headline on top and it takes them right into all the information so they either have a thank you page or they have a sales letter.

A thank you page just says thank you please check your email for your confirmation and you'll get the tele-class or the report that you signed up for.

If you just have the thank you page then you're missing the opportunity to have them deepen the relationship with you by investing in your offer. If you take them right to the sales page it's not acknowledging the steps they've already taken and acknowledgment is important. So in the initial sales letter I have just a few lines at the top saying congratulations on requesting, whatever this free thing they requested was, please check your email you'll get that in a minute, in the meantime check this out. There's this little transition that acknowledges that they've taken action and invites them to go deeper into your world and that just feels good to me.

With List-a-Palooza I keep making decisions around what I feel really awesome about putting out into the world, like this feels good for me to offer. If somebody says I don't like the way you did that I don't worry about it because I feel so good about it. Whereas if I did something the way my mentor told me to do and then, if somebody said I didn't like it, I'd be like "I know I'm horrible!" Instead of having that, I believe in standing strong in myself and in my value and putting my best out there into the world.

Things That Don't Work

One of things that I have done that has not worked is investing in paid advertising without having a good way to track it. When I first found out about Facebook, it seemed like a good idea. But I didn't have any tracking links to see exactly how many people were coming to the page, how many of those people were opting in and how many of those people were buying something so I basically just threw money down the toilet. That didn't work very well; in addition my ads were not targeted well. Another mistake I made was not having a little crazy, easy yes offer right there immediately once they sign up. When you have that in place it allows you to recoup some or all of your investment from paid advertising right away. What some people do is they'll use Facebook ads to fill their webinar or their event or their tele-class and that's great, I'm not saying don't do that but the scary part of it is they don't know until after the tele-class if it worked. What I like about having a little offer right after the option page is that you know immediately what's working and what's not.

I'll test a bunch of different ads, I'll say okay here's ad one, two, three, four, five and within a day or two I know which ones are working and which ones aren't. I end up paying one to two dollars per opt in where other people are paying more like $5 per opt in, because they haven't had the opportunity to test it. By the time they get the results it's done, they can't go back and make changes because the launch has finished.

A few advertising things I have done that haven't worked very well for me are, number one doing a re-targeting campaigns which means that when somebody visits your page whether they opt in or not, your banner ads follow them all over the internet. I thought wow my ads are going to be following people everywhere, they're going to see me everywhere it's going to absolutely amazing. It was fun people were like "oh my God I just saw your ad on this site that's so cool", but I can't say that it really paid off financially. I haven't given up on re-targeting but I think when I do it again I will need to be more involved in the process. I had hired someone to do it for me and I believe I need to do more testing and tweaking myself before I outsource it again.

Another thing that I tried was advertising on someone's blog, it's like $100 a month to have a little link on her blog, she's got a lot of traffic going to her blog but it wasn't necessarily my ideal clients, it was just this random smattering of humanity. I think it might have worked better if I advertised on somebody else's blog, because basically I just took $100 and burned it. I didn't feel bad about it because I was willing to put this $100 out there and see how it goes. The thing that I did well there was I tracked it.

It totally worked out in terms of figuring out what works and what doesn't. It's kind of like when people tend to say hey you know you've failed, nine thousand times it's like no, no, no I'm just successfully finding nine thousand things that don't work!

Jumpstart The Process

The idea that continues to call me forward when everything gets hard is that your people are waiting for you. This concept has gotten me through the real estate crash, the learning curve of internet marketing and many other challenges I've run up against. I stop making it about me and I focus on the people that I'm meant to serve. For example I went to eight different chiropractors before I found this one chiropractor that makes all the difference, when he adjusts with me it's just much more transformative than the other people, I've had the same experience with massage therapists. I've had the same experience with mentors and coaches and speakers. There are some people who I could listen to all day and every time they open their mouths my world transforms they give me great ideas, I implement them, they work. There are other people who I know they're really the same but I'm just not feeling it.

If you've ever had an experience like that, I would say that every person has their own healers, teachers, mentors and if you can see that it's true for you that's evidence that the reverse is also true. If you have your own speakers, healers and teachers that just give it to you the way you get it, like my people come up and tell me, oh my God I've heard this before but now that you've said it I get it, now I take action, now I'm getting results, you are speaking to me the way that I need to learn. That's great, that means those are my people, I'm their teacher. If you've had that experience that means that you are also the healer, the teacher, the mentor for someone else and if you don't show up then they're not going to get the healing and the transformation that they need. So that's the thought I would like to leave you with is to show up for your people and building a big email list, going out there building a business that is a way to expand your message, make a bigger difference in the world whether all of those people sign up for your offerings or not.

DOING THINGS DIFFERENT

When you are confronted with, "Wow this feels really big or this feels like a stretch, instead of saying to yourself, "I can't do it," what if you went, "How can I?" Listen in to see what each of our speakers does different!
http://crackingtheclientattractioncode.com

CHAPTER FIVE

Your Invisible Family Entanglements and Childhood Imprints are Holding You Back

By Dana Garrison, MSW, MFEW
CEO and Founder
Business Consultant, Success Coach, Family Entanglement Expert, Author
President Entrepreneur and Small Business Institute

"Whether you think you can or you think you can't, you're right."
— Henry Ford

How I Came Into My Calling

How did I come into my calling? I was actually in my teens when I discovered my purpose. I saw how much needless pain, suffering and injustice existed in the world and made it my mission to create as much positive change on the planet as I could.

Over the years I figured out that if I help people who will contribute to the world in some way, and if I help people who will be making a difference in some way, then I could have an exponential effect and create ripples of positive change for the planet. But I didn't know specifically how I was going to help people when I first started. I just had the knowing that I wanted to.

Then in my early twenties, I contracted a mystery illness that no doctor could diagnose. It gave me chronic fatigue, insomnia, memory loss, depression, anxiety, and hair loss. It gave me trouble reading, writing, speaking, and even thinking. It was debilitating and extremely frightening especially because I didn't know what was happening to me. I saw a lot of specialists in western medicine, eastern medicine, energy medicine, and alternative medicine but no one could diagnose nor even relieve the symptoms.

Eventually I realized that I just needed to get on with life as best I could, and I had learned that even if you don't know exactly what you want to do yet, just take a step, learn from that step, and keep moving forward. Stay in action. So I became a therapist because it seemed like a great way to help people. Yet despite all the therapy tools, I still found that some people weren't getting the breakthroughs that they wanted. In fact some people were in therapy for ten to twenty years and were still not getting all the results they wanted in life. This troubled me – I thought, there must be a better way.

Then one day, I discovered something that would change the very course of my life; I learned that the "results" we have in our lives, things like our health, our income, our career, our relationships (or lack thereof), or the state of our business, are **90% determined by our unconscious patterns**. Only 10% of what we have in life is determined by our conscious thoughts and decisions! That was a huge turning point for me and I began searching for answers in the realm of addressing our unconscious patterns.

Over the years, I dove into this field and learned many different methods and modalities that were meant to clear out our unconscious patterns and mindsets. Some worked a little, some didn't seem to work at all, and a few stood out. I took the best of the best elements from different types of transformational work and I developed something called Family Entanglement Work, and Childhood Re-Imprinting.

I tried this work on myself first, and did sessions to address the chronic fatigue. The deep level of fatigue I felt just disappeared. I was blown away. So I tried it on the anxiety next because it was causing me to feel a lot of stress and overwhelm, and that just went away and never came back. This work was getting rid of many of the symptoms that had haunted me for a decade, and that no doctor or specialist could help me with. In the end, it helped me finally get a diagnosis too. Naturally, I fell in love with it.

I took this work to my clients, too, and in the places where they had been stuck for years, sometimes their whole lives, they began to shift, and people were finally getting the breakthroughs that they wanted and had sometimes waited their whole lives for. I was stunned and fascinated.

I became an even bigger fan of this work when I saw that the two main culprits that were holding pretty much all of my clients back seemed to be their Family Entanglements and Childhood Imprints. When I worked with these, I was getting to the root cause of their problems, and was able to help create bigger, faster, and long-lasting breakthroughs.

So What Are Family Entanglement and Childhood Imprints?

Family Entanglements are the problems and patterns that we inherit from previous generations around money, business, relationships, health, and happiness.

Childhood Imprints are the problems and patterns that we get "imprinted" with between conception and age seven – our Imprint Period.

As I began to use this work with myself and my clients, I began to wonder, what types of problems could this work help to resolve?

If I could use this work to address health issues and topics that came up in therapy, could I also use this work to address income and growing a business?

At the time, I was working 9-5 as a therapist and unfortunately I was in a toxic work environment. It was making my health get worse again and I knew I had to get out. I realized that I was going to have to work for myself.

So I got the idea to try using the Family Entanglement Work and Childhood Re-Imprinting to address any business blocks and income blocks that I had, and what happened after that blew me away; I was able to have a sold out coaching practice in one and a half months, and then grow my business to six figures in nine months. That really shocked me and of course, I began to help clients with their business and income breakthroughs using this work as well.

When I saw how powerful Family Entanglement Work and Childhood Re-Imprinting was, I realized that this could help thousands of people free themselves from their inner blocks and the core of what was holding them back so that they could start living the lives that they truly wanted.

This is what I had been looking for, for so many years, to help create positive change on the planet. I realized when I can free people to live their best life, or to realize their dreams, their mission, their purpose, then the positive effect would be exponential. As they began to live the lives they wanted and as they were able to live their purpose, or have the business or career they wanted, they would be able to contribute to the world in a way that resonated with them and take care of those they loved. I realized that when I helped one person, it would create a positive ripple effect by affecting everyone else in their life.

It was through my own struggle with health and business, and my own journey and breakthroughs that I was able to find my calling and be able to do this work for others.

What Makes This Work Different

I grew to realize that there are so many trainings, therapies, and healing modalities out there that only address the symptoms of a problem. It's like having a garden full of weeds and most of the solutions out there are just like lawnmowers. They mow down the tops of the weeds, but the weeds just keep coming back. Doing Family Entanglement Work and Childhood Re-Imprinting is like getting out those weeds by the root. In fact, I collectively call Childhood Re-Imprinting and Family Entanglement Work "Core Cause Work" because it gets right to the root cause and addresses the problem at its core, right at the source. That's why the transformation in people is long lasting and that's what makes this work unique.

When you have a problem that you just can't seem to get rid of...something that follows you, something that haunts you, that's indicative of an Imprint or Entanglement at play. This is especially true if you've tried something in the past to address the problem, like attending a class or training, reading a book on the topic, or doing some kind of therapy or healing work and the problem still sticks or re-occurs.

Over the years, I've seen that Core Cause Work is able to address the toughest of problems and patterns in life and finally give people the breakthroughs they've been waiting (sometimes way too long) for. Having a mystery illness showed me that life is short. Tomorrow isn't promised. Next month isn't promised. So I believe in working towards living the life that we want to live, right now, and being able to start getting traction, and getting shifts and changes we want sooner rather than later.

On Business

I'll share with you some of the ways that I've attracted clients and what I've noticed and learned about how that attraction works. The ability to attract clients is actually of utmost importance to the health and survival of anyone's business.

Probably the biggest thing that I've witnessed that gets in the way of being able to attract clients is a person's Imprints and Entanglements and here's why: we as humans are constantly communicating with each other unconsciously. What I mean is, our unconscious is continuously blaring silent messages to others anytime we're around other people. Whether we are communication is through writing, like when you're writing copy for your website or an ad that you're placing; when you're speaking, either to a group or just to an individual; even when you're just sitting in the same room with someone, your unconscious is sending out messages. No matter the context or scenario, you're always unconsciously communicating with others around you.

Something that many of us don't realize is that our unconscious communication is much louder than our conscious communication. When you have a Childhood Imprint of "I'm not good enough or I'm not important" or "Money's hard to get," other people are unconsciously picking up on those messages. They won't necessarily consciously know why, but they just won't be attracted to you, or they wont' want to work with you or buy your product. Their conscious mind might come up with some explanation or excuse, like "Well, I don't have enough money right now," or "I don't have time for this right now," or "I don't know, I'm just not resonating with this." But underneath the surface explanation, they are actually reacting to the unconscious messages you're projecting, and their conscious mind is simply coming up with a rationale.

The same goes for Family Entanglements. Let me give you an example: if you have the Entanglements called No Permission for Success or No Permission for Abundance, your unconscious won't have permission to allow success in.

This is one of the major sources of self-sabotage. If you've ever noticed that you've accidentally or purposefully self-sabotaged, the first place you want to look is your Entanglements and Imprints. These two culprits are famous for creating a lack of internal permission to have success.

In all my years of working with people and helping them grow their businesses, I've learned that Imprints and Entanglements are the main blocks for attracting the clients you want. When I help entrepreneurs, I help them with business mentoring and business strategy, like improving their sales and marketing, and I also work with Inner Game, their Imprints and Entanglements. Through the years I've noticed that what's actually holding people back more than anything is their Imprints and Entanglements.

A very important thing to note is that Entanglements and Imprints aren't your fault. You develop Imprints when you are just a child and you get them because your brain is looking to make sense of the world as fast as possible so you can survive. And Entanglements are often passed down from generation to generation through the unconscious and through your Epigenomes, which are part of your DNA.

I'll share more about how Imprints and Entanglement are created and how we get them in the online course I'll give you as a gift, but for now, the important thing to know is that they are not your fault. The struggles you've had in your life often make perfect sense once you see what your Entanglements and Imprints are – they perfectly align. And the good news is you aren't stuck with them. You can be freed of your Entanglements and Imprints, and you can have the breakthroughs and the life you want.

Go here to the Gifts from Contributors chapter to register for the online course for free.

Fascinating Facts about Family Entanglements

Family Entanglements are the problems and patterns that are passed down from generation to generation. These patterns get passed down for up to seven generations before they fade out, and you're often most deeply affected by the last three generations. That means the relatives in your parent's generation, your grandparent's generation, and your great grandparent's generation are the ones from which you inherit the most.

So if someone from a previous generation struggled or suffered a tragedy or a trauma in their life, around money, business, relationship, or health, then that can become an **Originating Incident** that sets off an **Entanglement Pattern**. As Entanglements travel down the generations, they don't always take the same exact same form.

Let's take a look at a Money Entanglement, just to give you an example. Let's say that your grandfather lived through the Great Depression and he lost the family's savings. That's painful and it changes him. It changes his core thoughts, feelings, and beliefs around money and survival. He can begin to feel that money is scarce, money is hard to get, money is hard to keep, money doesn't stay.

Then along comes your dad. Let's say that your dad gets entangled with this Money Entanglement. As the Entanglement moves down the generations, the way it gets expressed can vary, even though the topic stays the same. So the topic of this Entanglement is money, but perhaps your Dad's version of the Money Entanglement is that he goes bankrupt.

Then you come along and maybe you get entangled with this. Your variation of the Money Entanglement is that you struggle to grow your business and you're not making enough money. Perhaps you find that you have a Money Ceiling. A **Money Ceiling** is when you seem to be able to make or save a certain amount of money per month, and then once you begin to go above that amount, somehow you start to attract new and unexpected bills... medical bills, dental bills, maybe a car repair, or a home repair. You might end up with a speeding ticket, or a parking ticket, or some fees come in from the bank or the library, or the kids suddenly need something. That's when you know that you've got a Money Ceiling. You're only able to make or save a certain amount of money, and once you start to go above that amount, it doesn't last and something inevitably comes up and sucks the money away.

The funny thing is, you can inherit these patterns even if you never knew anything about your relatives, or never met them or even heard about them. That's because these patterns are passed down in a number of ways. One way is through the Unconscious Mind. Like I said earlier, our unconscious minds are always in communication with each other. We're constantly picking up information from our family members' unconscious patterns.

Another way that these patterns are passed down is through epigenetics. Epigenomes sit above your genes and tell your genes to switch on or switch off. Epigenomes are affected by the stressors in a person's life. So yes, the large emotional stresses that we go through effect our DNA. When you have a big, painful experience around money, that has an effect on your DNA and that can get passed down through generations. That means that you don't have to consciously know anything about certain family member, or their life, or their history, and you can still get entangled with their problems and patterns.

I'll share some examples of common Entanglements and some of the Originating Incidences that kick off that Entanglement Pattern in a family (this is a partial list):

No Permission for Abundance – this one gets started when someone in your family tree lost a lot of money, or gambled it away, or loaned it out and it didn't come back, or was blackmailed or backstabbed around money. It can make it so that growing your business or your income is challenging.

No Permission for Success – this one gets started when someone in your family tree failed a business, or didn't get to do what they loved. It can make you struggle with your own successes in your business or at your job.

No Permission for Connection – this one gets started when someone in your family tree didn't get to marry someone they loved (due to arranged marriage, or being from different religions, or classes or races, or the family forbid it), or they lost their partner (in an accident, for example) or if someone ended up closing off their heart or putting walls up around himself/herself. This can block your ability to find love, and have happy, lasting relationships. It can also prevent your business or career from growing.

Pull Towards Death - this one gets started when someone in your family tree died under the age of 25, if a parent died while they had children under the age of 15, if someone had a miscarriage, abortion, or still born, and if someone had a tragic fate. This one is an "all-arounder" – if you have this Entanglement, it can affect your income, your business/career, your relationships, your health and your happiness.

For a more complete list of Originating Incidences that kick off Entanglement Patterns, or Signs and Symptoms in your own life that show you're Entangled, sign up for the online course I'm gifting you for free and you'll not only get the course, you'll get a report on Family Entanglements that will help you uncover which ones you may have. You can register using the link in the Gifts from Contributors Chapter.

Intriguing Facts About Childhood Imprints

Childhood Imprints are patterns that you pick up in your childhood. You imprint thoughts, feeling and behavioral patterns about money, success, relationships, health, and happiness. Your Imprint Period is approximately between conception and age seven. That's when your brain is extremely malleable and it's trying so hard to imprint information about yourself and about life to try to ensure your survival.

So that means that there is such a thing as Fetal Imprints. Think back to what you know about your mom when she was pregnant with you. What was your mother probably going through, mentally, emotionally and physically? What was she probably thinking, feeling, or experiencing?

This is one of the ways we develop **Imprinted Emotions** – which are the emotions you are guaranteed to feel every week of the year. So in any given calendar week of the year, if it is common for you to feel anxiety, frustration, stress, worry, overwhelm, sadness, doubt, jealousy, or any other negative emotion, you've found one of your Imprinted Emotions.

The other type of Imprint is your Childhood Imprints. There are three major types of Childhood Imprints. There are **Identity Imprints**, Imprints about yourself; **Relational Imprints**, Imprints about what people are going to be like and what relationships are going to be like; and there's **Global Imprints,** which express what life and the world in general is going to be like.

And whatever you imprint, you tend to attract to yourself, or create for yourself, over and over again.

So some questions worth asking yourself are:

What messages were you receiving about yourself when you were growing up?

What messages did you get from caretakers, siblings, teachers and peers?

Here's a list of some of the most common Imprints about yourself:

1. **I'm not good enough** [I don't have what it takes]
2. **I'm not smart enough** [I'm stupid / I'm dumb when it comes to _____]
3. **I don't belong** [I'm an outsider/outcast/black sheep]
4. **I'm a bad person** [I'm not a good person / I do bad things]
5. **There's something wrong with me** [I'm missing something / I'm not ok]
6. **I'm not important** [I don't matter]
7. **I'm a quitter** [I don't finish what I start]
8. **I don't deserve _____** [I don't deserve to receive _____ / I'm undeserving]
9. **I'm unlovable** [I'm not _____ enough to be loved/lovable]
10. **I fail** [I screw things up / I make a mess of _____ / I'm a screw up]
11. **I'm not worthy** [I'm worthless / I don't count]
12. **I'm unwanted** [It would be better if I wasn't here]

13. **I'm a phony** [I'm a fake (and it's going to be found out)]

14. **I can't be seen** [It's better to stay small / I should be/need to be invisible]

15. **I'm not safe** [I can't relax / I feel vulnerable / I can't let my guard down]

Those are just some examples of Identity Imprints that you can pick up. You can probably see how these can get in the way of success, relationships and health.

Then of course there are the Relational and Global Imprints, Imprints about people and life. These govern what types of people, situations and circumstances you attract and create in your life.

Some examples of Relational and Global Imprints:

1. **It's not safe** [People aren't safe / Life isn't safe]

2. **I have to do it all by myself** [I can't trust others to do it/ do it right]

3. **Life is hard** [Life is a struggle]

4. **I'm alone** [People don't stay / It's hard to find a partner / People abandon you]

5. **People can't be trusted** [People are generally untrustworthy]

6. **Money is hard to get** [Money is hard to earn]

7. **Money is hard to keep** [Money is hard to save / Money doesn't stay]

8. **There's not enough** [There's not enough _____]

9. **Intimacy is dangerous** [Letting someone get close is dangerous / People will use things against you]

10. **People aren't reliable** [I can't rely on others to _____]

11. **People will only love me if I'm good** [People will only give me attention if I do well / People will only be attracted to me if I seem perfect / I need to be perfect]

12. **I can't be myself and be loved** [To fit in I have to be like others / I have to change myself around people to fit in]

There are also other categories of Imprints, such as Money Imprints, which affect your income and your business. To get a more complete list, sign up for the online course I'm gifting you for free and you'll get a report on Childhood Imprints. Find the registration link in the Gifts from Contributors chapter.

What Inspires Customers to Say "Yes" to You

One of the strongest influences to getting a "yes" from a possible customer is being a "yes" inside you. You want to be aligned with people saying yes to you, and that means consciously aligned *and* unconsciously aligned. And the latter is the tougher part.

Our Entanglements and Imprints can act as an unconscious "no." They send negative messages to prospective clients without us even knowing it's happening. That's because it's all happening unconsciously and silently. Entanglement and Imprints can act like invisible puppet strings pulling us this way and that.

Now keep in mind that consciously, we can be the yes. We may be thinking with our conscious mind – "I really need the money right now," or "I'm a yes to this person," or "I really like this person; I'd like to work with them," or "I've got space in my practice right now, come right in!" But like I said, our conscious thoughts only have a 10% effect on the total outcome. The most important place to be a yes is in the 90% of what's really in charge of your results and that means addressing anything that doesn't allow us to be a yes in our unconscious patterning.

One of the most compelling places where you can inspire a client to say yes is when you're having a conversation with them about working with you. Perhaps you give free consultations or have a presentation that you do. These are great places to be inspiring and to connect with a prospect and invite them to try your service or product. And this is one of the most powerful places where you want to have your unconscious be aligned with a "yes."

I'll share an example. I had a client named Mary and when she came to me she said she had resistance to giving these free consults. She reported that she felt uncomfortable with talking about what she did, offering her service, and talking about money. She would avoid having those calls and conversations. She would procrastinate, and that was part of her self-sabotage. And of course, she didn't get enough customers and her business didn't grow.

When I looked into her family tree, I saw that her brother didn't get his fair share of the family inheritance. That is one of the incidences that can happen in a family that causes the 'No Permission for Abundance' Entanglement. Once we disentangled her from that, she reported to me that she felt so much ease with getting on the phone and making call after call and having these conversations. She said it was so comfortable, in fact, that it felt as if she was talking to her best friend. Now that's a 180 degree shift she had, and it wasn't because she learned something new in business. It was because she addressed the No Permission for Abundance Entanglement: that was to root cause of her resistance to making those calls.

Now if you asked her, she wouldn't have been able to tell you that it was the Entanglement that was the root cause. She thought she was uncomfortable with talking about what she did, putting herself out there, and having money conversations. But in reality, the Entanglement was the root cause, because after we disentangled her, without additional business training, she simply found that the inner resistance and uncomfortable feelings disappeared.

Imagine thinking that the reason you're stuck is because of something that you feel uncomfortable with, or don't feel good at, only to discover that the real reason is an unconscious block. And imagine removing that unconscious block and getting unstuck, starting to feel more and more ease and freedom. That's what I love about this work – it gets you unstuck from those places that you thought were your fault, or you thought was bad luck, and you come to find it wasn't you or bad luck at all, it was just an Entanglement or Imprint, and you can clear those out.

Things That Should Work But Often Don't

One of the biggest things that doesn't work is thinking that you need to take more business training. Don't get me wrong. You need business training. Everyone needs business training if they're going to be in business. But when something isn't working, to try to take more business training, or to simply try something different in business is not generally the answer.

I've actually found that you can take numerous business trainings and read multiple books, and hire a coach or mentor, but if you haven't addressed your Entanglements and Imprints yet, then all those business techniques and tools may not work, even if you're "doing them right."

And that's because if you haven't addressed your Inner Game yet, there's likely unconscious blocks to your success that need to be cleared out. And luckily, clearing them out is rather fun and simple.

In essence, what *doesn't* work is focusing only on your Outer Game - business training and business knowledge - without addressing your Inner Game - the unconscious blocks that hold you back from getting what you want.

You need to have both. Think of it this way. Your Outer Game - business training and knowledge - is like having power tools. Your Inner Game is the electricity that makes those power tools work. You can have all the tools you want but if they're not plugged in, you're going to struggle.

When people address their Inner Game and remove their unconscious blocks, they report being able to do the things they want to do in their business (and their life), and they report being able to get customers and grow their income with much more at ease. They also report living their day to day much more in their A-Game. Imagine your day unfolding with more flow, and being able to do what you want (or need) to do with more ease. Imagine having more customers wanting to talk to you and wanting to purchase your services or products. How would that change your business and your life?

The other thing that doesn't work that I see a lot of, is blaming yourself for what's not going well and thinking that it means you aren't smart enough, or don't have what it takes to be successful. And it's easy to end up blaming ourselves because we are the ones who are experiencing the pain of feeling stuck. Many of us have heard that we are supposedly 100% responsible for what's showing up in our lives. Well, that's not quite the whole truth.

In fact, there's a deeper truth - we have Entanglements and Imprints that shape us and affect us. They also tend to prevent us from getting what we want. Entanglements and Imprints are part of the human experience; we all share in that. And they aren't your fault. Today we're drawing a line in the sand: The blame stops here. Toady I'm going to encourage you to stop blaming yourself for the things that you've been struggling with. To stop thinking that you don't have what it takes, or aren't good enough. The things that you've been struggling with are often because of your Entanglements and Imprints. Blaming yourself doesn't make sense, because it's not you, it's the Entanglements and Imprints that are holding you back.

Second of all, blaming yourself brings down your energy and brings down your confidence and you're A-Game. And when you are not feeling confident, when you're in you're A-Game, and you feel more stressed, or uncertain, when you're feeling negative or have lost your confidence, many things start to crumble. So it doesn't work in your favor to blame yourself. And it's not the truth anyway. So draw the line in the sand. The blame stops today.

On Health

When I came to this work, I had my first amazing breakthroughs around health. Any kind of health problems that you or your loved ones have struggled with are often intimately tied to Entanglements and Imprints. Some of the symptoms of the Mystery Illness included anxiety and depression. When I looked into my family tree, I noticed that there were a lot of young deaths in my family. I'm half Taiwanese and my grandmother lost two children when they were just babies. She felt a lot of anxiety and pain, and it was exhausting. That is a common type of Originating Incident that kicks off the Pull Towards Death Entanglement. As that Entanglement trickled down the generations, it affected my mom, and she had 2 miscarriages and she experienced a lot of anxiety and depression. Then I got entangled with it and I came down with a Mystery Illness that no doctor could diagnose, but two of the symptoms that came with the disease were anxiety and depression. I went to so many doctors, western, eastern, alternative, and no one was able to diagnose me or heal me. I was also able to address the severe fatigue that came with the Mystery Illness by addressing the Pull Towards Death Entanglement. Health is everything; if you don't have your health, you can't really have a successful business, and it can get in the way of your relationships. So health is a vital element that you have to protect or your entire life can get turned upside down.

On Relationships

Even though people tend to come to me to work on business success and money breakthroughs, people often also want to work on their relationships. They want to improve their current relationship or find their soul mate. In terms of relationships, you can have Imprints that block your ability to attract and sustain a loving, juicy, passionate relationship. Here's a few example Imprints that can get in the way:

I'm unlovable

I don't deserve love

I'm unworthy

I'm not good enough

I'm not important

I'm alone

I don't belong

These Childhood Imprints absolutely block juicy, yummy, delicious relationships from coming into your life or from existing in your life.

There's a particular Entanglement that is famous for affects relationships, and that's the No Permission for Connection Entanglement. This one will prevent you from being able to attract a compatible partner into your life or a soul mate. If you are currently in a relationship, this Entanglement can also be the one that causes a lot of strife and struggle and arguments. It can also affect your friendships, and your relationships with your co-workers, bosses, and your family members.

Of course, it means that it also affects your business relationships too. When you've got the Entanglements and Imprints that block connection, then your prospective clients can end up feeling less excited about you, less attracted to working with you or buying your product. Like I said earlier, they won't quite know why, but they can feel that it's hard to fully connect with you, or feel completely committed to working with you, or they simply just don't feel sold on your product or service. So if you have the No Permission for Connection Entanglement, it's one you want to address.

Again, to see which Entanglements and Imprints are affecting you, go to the chapter called Gifts from Contributors and get a free course on Entanglements and Imprints.

On Happiness

The last topic for us to explore is happiness. If your mood or emotional state is negative in some way, if you tend to get into a state of frustration, or stress, or overwhelm, or anxiety fairly frequently, then it's likely that you'll attract struggle and roadblocks into your life.

Let's take a moment and talk about Imprinted Emotions. You'll recall from earlier that an Imprinted Emotion is an emotion that you are guaranteed to feel in any calendar week of the year. If you are guaranteed to feel sad, or disappointed, or frustrated, or anxious, then those are your Imprints Emotions. Trying to run a business or grow a business in states of stress, or overwhelm, or anxiety, or worry is not conducive to success. It's so much harder and it slows down your progress. It attracts struggle and you can end up attracting difficult clients or clients you don't want to work with because of the state that you're emanating and that you exist in.

So it's important to address your negative Imprinted Emotions, so that they don't keep bringing about struggle or difficulty in the areas of life that are important to you. And at the very least, we want to address them because they create a less pleasant experience of life, and there's no point in living that way when clearing these out is practical and simple.

Imagine being free of those stuck emotions. Imagine being able to feel the emotions that you like more often. What would that do for your relationships? Your career or business? Your health?

When You Clear Your Entanglements and Imprints

When it comes to business, people come to me because they want to grow their business, get more customers, increase their income, and the like. I'll share some quick stories from people who have worked on their Entanglements and Imprints around money and business so you can have a deeper sense of how Imprints and Entanglements affect our lives and what results can look like.

I worked with a woman named Alyssa. She was a Pilates instructor and had been attempting to grow her business for almost a year. She walked up to me after I got off stage at a live event, and she was crying. She said "I don't know if I'm cut out for business. I just don't think I can do it. I've been trying for almost a year now and it's just not happening." I'm sure some of us can relate to this.

I asked her some questions about her family and I found out that she was actually entangled with her father who had lost a lot of money. We worked together and disentangled her from the No Permission for Abundance Entanglement. Within two weeks, she attracted more clients than she had in the nine months previous. And she didn't do anything different. She didn't call anybody. She didn't place an ad. She didn't do a workshop. People just started walking in to her classes, and contacting her and wanting to sign up. She ended up with a wait-list of new clients. She actually had to put people on a wait-list because so many new customers showed up unexpectedly.

Now that's a great "problem" to have! When we addressed her unconscious lack of permission for money to come in, she began emanating a different "energy" because her unconscious was open to getting new customers. And people can feel that. Imagine people becoming more drawn to working with you because something inside of you finally feels okay with receiving more money. It makes such a big difference. We often don't realize just how powerful out Inner Game is when it comes to making more money or getting more clients.

I worked with another woman, named Jasmine, who had two elderly care facilities. One of the problems she was facing was that when there weren't enough clients in the center, she still had to pay for all the workers and the rent and all the electricity and other bills. She came to me because one of her centers was empty.

I looked in her family tree and I saw that her father actually had trouble in his business. He was a door-to-door salesman, and he would make sales, but he never went back to collect the money and complete the order. He was uncomfortable with money. Of course, he was not successful with his business and Jasmine was entangled with him. This is the no Permission for Success and No Permission for Abundance Entanglements working hand in hand. When we did some sessions and disentangled her from her dad, within about one or two months, both centers were completely full. She went from having a five figure business to a six figure business (over $100,000 a year).

When someone else in our family didn't succeed, we can get entangled with that pattern and we can pick up an unconscious sense that block permission for success or abundance.

I'll share a couple stories about Imprints as well, so you have a sense of how they work.

I worked with a gentleman named Bill, who's a financial planner. He had a number of Childhood Imprints, one of which was "I'm a phony and I'm going to be found out." He had a tendency to feel like things weren't going to work out, and he often experienced a sense of dread. That was an old Imprint from childhood. After we worked together and addressed his Imprints, his business went from a five figure business to a multiple six figure business (over $200,000 a year). He was able to be home more often to be with his two young daughters, to be there for their soccer games, and to take more vacations. Imagine being able to have more ease and have more time and money. What would you do with that? What are some of the things that are close to your heart that you would spend more time doing?

The last example I'll share is a gentleman named Merrill. He always had five figure jobs. He had come to me and said "Dana, I want make six figures finally! I want to break through." He had a lot of learning disabilities his whole life, and the "I'm not good enough" Imprint haunted him. He also had the "I'm not Important" and "I'm not Smart Enough" Imprints. He joined Freedom Tribe – the weekly group where I help people Disentangle and Re-Imprint and within about 4 months, he not only attracted but landed his first six-figure job.

So you see how the Inner Game is so intimately tied to what we are able to attract and what we are able to manifest or create in our lives. Those are some real world examples of how this work works, and what transformation can look like.

I created a gift for those of you who are reading this - to help you get some relief and some breakthroughs in your own life. The first step to freeing yourself is your awareness - knowing which Entanglements and Imprints are affecting you is literally half the battle. So I've created a course, which I'll give you as a gift.

This awareness will help you see how the struggles you've faced aren't your fault, and that you can be free of them. It will also help you address your Entanglements and Imprints because once you can see which one you have, they can't hide in the darkness anymore. Once you have awareness, they don't have the power they use to anymore.

So many people have told me that when they have an awareness of their Entanglements and Imprints, it is a transformative experience, and a very valuable one. Shifts and changes just start showing up in their lives. And they feel more empowered and have more control over how they feel, what happens in their relationships, and what happens in their business or career. Simply knowing your Entanglements and Imprints to crumble the structures that hold the Family Entanglements and Childhood I in place.

And I'll be giving doing some sessions for you in the online course as well, so you will also get to address some of your Entanglements and Imprints right at the root. Many people have written to me and expressed how much they enjoyed the course and how much value they've gotten from it, and have shared their breakthroughs with me. I want to invite you to do the same, so I can celebrate your shifts and breakthroughs with you.

To see which Entanglements and Imprints are affecting you, to have conscious mind and unconscious mind breakthroughs, and to experience some sessions, go to the Gifts from Contributors chapter and you can get the online course on Entanglements and Imprints for free.

ARE YOU READY FOR YOUR BREAKTHROUGH?

Listen to the interview with Dana Garrison. She will guide you through a mini session where you will work on some stuff around money, your congruency, your permission for more money to come in. http://crackingtheclientattractioncode.com

---

CHAPTER SIX

Shining The Light On Growth Potential

BY TRACEY FIEBER
Founder Tracey Fieber Business Solutions
Business Expert & Speaker

Innovation is the specific instrument of entrepreneurship. The act that endows resources with a new capacity to create wealth.

— Peter Drucker

To be honest, I never actually 'discovered my calling', it's been evolving. When I was in the corporate world I worked at a financial institution for fifteen years. During that time, the last eight years I was manager of Marketing, Operations and Human Resources. I loved my job, but I also found that because I was doing it for one company the new projects kept me engaged, and when there wasn't a new project I started to get bored. When you're working in the financial industry you do see a lot of other businesses. I started to notice what wasn't going well for the businesses. Then I realized if I could do for the other companies what I do for this one financial institution, I could really make a difference in the world. When I quit my job, there were a lot of different reasons why I quit but this was one of the main ones. I was also getting more and more sick and I couldn't seem to get myself out of it. I knew that it wasn't necessarily the job; it was me that was making myself sick. So I needed to make changes. I quit my job much to the surprise of all of the people in the whole system, but it was something that I felt I needed to do. This was when I discovered my calling, that's exactly what it was... it was a calling to say "okay Tracey, now is the time. If you don't make a change now you're not going to make it to sixty five let alone teaching people or helping them to invest, once they are sixty five and retired.

From Retirement Transition to Business Development

While I was in the financial institution I had that calling, but I didn't necessarily pay attention to it. When I started my business, I started helping people in their retirement transition, because I felt that was part of my calling. As I did that I noticed that the people who were coming to me were typically business owners and they were looking for retirement transition help. But they were looking to set up their businesses so that they could either sell it or have it run without them. Once I started to notice that and really pay attention to it, I had ah-ha' moment and I wondered if

I marketed that... what would happen? And you know the rest is history.

I've had some great coaches along the way, people who've given me a sense of direction and helped me put things into place. My business grew because it is important to get the bases set up which is really what we did for ourselves, thank goodness. Many companies do this for other people but don't necessarily do it for themselves at first. We've been really conscious of doing this and advising other people too. We've got a great team of people and we've got an office building now.

I started first in my kitchen at home, in my home office and now we've expanded to an office with six people along with us. We have a virtual team as well who does some work for us, and we hire other outsourcers, other consultants and experts for certain areas of the business. I would rather pay somebody who is an expert to do it rather than have to take the slow way. Having said that, there are times that I will then bring it in-house once things are set up and running. Bringing it in house almost always saves money.

So you should always be looking at how you can set up your business to really keep more of the profit that you make. And you are certainly going to be re-investing in your business, but really pay attention all along to that calling. At first the retirement transition was my calling and it is still part of my business because of that. My calling is so much bigger, if I would have just stuck only with that then I wouldn't have been totally expressing myself. Now, I'm going into companies to help them set it up so they can get to that next stage in life.

I work with small, medium, and large companies. The large companies are having us come in and really do an organizational assessment to see what their areas of growth opportunities are. We shine a light in different area of business, including the areas of marketing, human resources and hiring, and staffing and team work. Where teamwork is concerned if you know somebody's not doing his or her job, you need to ask yourself "why do we need to get rid of that person? Is there actually something we can do and make some changes to help that person become more engaged or recommit?" In the area of marketing, whether it's online or traditional marketing we use all our theories ourselves in our business.

We find a lot of people really honour and appreciate that we're not just teaching the theory, we're teaching practical too. Our training actually involves having people learn the theory, and more importantly we give examples that relate to their own lives, and ask them for their own examples. That's really where we're different because we implement both for ourselves and for our clients.

The Transformation

It's just so awesome to see, the best reward is when that transformation happens. We have one client who we worked with three years ago. They sent me a testimonial letter to say thank you. She said, "we went from a mom and pop shop to being an actual growing concern business". They did not have to hire one position, they were actually able to cut one position, so it's not that they cut somebody and got rid of them, when the person left they just didn't fill it and they re-structured the work. We helped the business owner learn how to delegate so that things weren't piled up on her desk when she got back after vacation. They now take two months off every winter to go south because they want to. They hadn't had a holiday in years and now they can take two months off. When the return, the owner doesn't have stacks and stacks of things waiting for her and the business is still running and growing while she's gone. That kind of transformation is just so fulfilling...to be able to see the difference in someone's life.

It really technically gives them their life back because then they can start to enjoy life again. They're not working until ten, eleven, midnight, night after night, getting up early. Some of the people that we work with are getting along with just three to five hours sleep at night for long periods of time. Those are the kind of things that people will do in order to get a business up and running or keep a business running and yet I know that it's not necessary to be that way. Another company that we're working with has a dream to be able to have the business set up and have other partners come in on partial ownership. So they'll retain some ownership, but they want to move somewhere else. So we're setting up the business and assessing everyone, and the whole team is on board, because they're seeing that this is a great company and they want to retain that. They don't want to grow to the point where they lose that, but they want to grow. We have conversations about making sure that the family atmosphere is retained, even when it is a large company. That is possible, though many people assume that it's not. It IS possible. Does it take a conscious effort? Absolutely!!! And that's where we can come in and help.

On Attracting Clients

We use a variety of ways to attract clients. When I started my business I was always looking for more clients and I see a lot of other business owners looking for similar results. The question always is... "What is the one way that's going to bring in all these clients? Let me tell you that it's not one way. It's usually a combination of ways. One of the things that we find works is a combination of offline and online. We have direct mail which brings potential clients to a website which in turn brings them to our automated information. That's how we use a combination of offline and online. We set things up as much automated as we can but we're not afraid to use offline and online methods together. For example, we use Facebook.

There was an instance where a prospective client called me on-line and when I mentioned our Facebook page has over 225,000 likes, he said "Tracey you actually have over three hundred!" I was pleasantly surprised; I hadn't looked at the numbers for a little while. So that's the sort of thing that attracts clients. Now I've also had some people say to me, "okay Tracey, with three hundred thousand likes on your page, how many are you REALLY connected with?" I tell them that out of three hundred thousand I have enough reach and there are enough people that I'm connect-ed with that make a difference. So they're really asking me why would you build it to three hundred thousand, are you really that intimately close with three hundred thousand? And my answer is look it's just like me standing on a stage, a lot of people know me, I may not know everyone of them, but the right people will come up and stop and talk to me and say "Hey, I need your help" or "I have a question". It's the same thing when you have Facebook or any of the social media or any of the other things that you do. There's a certain portion of people who are just going to be watching what you're doing. There are others who are going to be action takers and take what you teach them in your free information that you're providing and then use it. And then there are others who say, "I like your information, I like that you are teaching us that, but I want you to do it for us". And that's the sort of clients that we want to be able to have. Those clients that take our information, learn from it and then tell me what a difference it made. I love to hear those stories. And yet we also want to work with the people who are really raising their hand to say, "Hey I need help, can you help me?"

Inspiring Clients to say YES

Make sure you ask for the business, it is one of the things that I had to remind myself to do and a lot of our clients have to be re-minded to do. ASK. The thing that really inspires clients with marketing is using their own words to communicate with them. When I say things like we do the hiring, we do the marketing, and we do human resources and we do operations it doesn't always have a meaning to most people. But when I then break it down to use their words, to say ... "you know when you're up in the middle of the night and you can't sleep because you're thinking about all the things at work? THAT'S what we help with."▢ At that point people are inspired to say yes. So I make sure that when I'm having a call or a conversation with a potential client, I'm taking notes. I'm writing down their words and I'm not filtering it with my impression of their words. I'm writing down their exact words because that's what we need to use when we market.

We also ask questions. When I was having a conversation with someone they said... "You know when you ask these three questions, I wasn't even really looking. But when you asked these three questions I said oh, I know that's for me." That's exactly what I want to do to attract the clients because then I know I've got the right clients.

What NOT to Do

Some things haven't worked? One thing most importantly is trying to do it myself. You know I actually woke up one night and I know it sounds silly but it was like an epiphany for me. It was a realization that I'm not supposed to do this all by myself. I'm supposed to have a team of people that helps me and it was a vision of a patchwork quilt. This epiphany for me was like... "Oh my gosh! It's just like a quilt... the squares on a quilt.... it's not even the squares... it's the actual threads inside each of those squares... it's not even the thread, it's a little piece of string... a partial piece of string, but it's fit together with the next one which then creates that big support which you can actually wrap around you and pull on and it doesn't come apart. I know that sounds kind of quirky, but honestly that's what I woke up with one night. If everyone in the world would just realize this, everything in the world would work so much better together. We all rely on each other. We're here to work together just like those threads or pieces of thread in a quilt. It makes sense. Don't try to do everything by yourself.

Another thing that doesn't work is taking a course and then trying to do everything exactly as the course says. It works to some degree, but you always need to pay attention to your own intuition and your own preferences. You need to put your own spin, your own impression on it. For example I've purchased courses. They walk me through, I put all of those things into place, and I'm a high implementer. I'm waiting and I'm expecting it to work. But it's not working like they said it was going to. The cause... I didn't personalize it, I didn't put 'me' into it. So I go back, and personalize it, the connection happens and it's personalized for me. And now I don't implement without doing that. Now when I take a course or a training or workshop or learn something new, or even have these epiphanies, I make sure that I put 'me' into it. That's what people connect to, the individuals within the company. They don't connect to the company.

I often talk to different people who are writing either hiring ads, or they're doing some marketing. Typically these ads or marketing says "I'm a great company, look at me, come see what I do, you know you should work with me". But that doesn't connect with people. So I tell them instead to write about what's important to the client, the words that they're using. Instead, you find yourself asking, "Is this your problem? Do you have trouble like this? Are you staying awake at night and wondering and worrying about where the next money is going to come from? We can help companies like that, we help companies to grow". That's the sort of thing for which people say to themselves... "Oh I want some of that!"

Social Marketing

There are lots of different social media platforms, marketing strategies and techniques out there. We do SEO for other companies, to help them get a good Google ranking. When somebody new comes to me I always ask, how you heard about us or where you found us. Mostly it's Google. Then sometimes one person says, well actually somebody else told me to take a look because you had this posted, so I took a look and then I Googled you. You have to make sure your search engine optimization; your search engine marketing is working for you.

Another social marketing platform that works well is LinkedIn. We routinely post on LinkedIn and really talk about the things that we're doing, or the problems our customers are having. Some people are apprehensive talking about what they're doing, or the problems that their customers are having. Yet it's what allows other people to connect, because they have similar problems. Even if it's not exactly the same they see themselves in that person's problem. Then they connect knowing full well that you are the right person to work with.

On the social marketing front, we also use Twitter, YouTube video, and Google Hang Outs. Most of the things we're either dabbling in or going for it full force. We're starting some Google Pay Per Click Ad Word campaigns and we've got some experts who have done this before. We've set a budget for how much we want to spend and then we're going to get it up and running, and then see how its working, keep a close eye on it. That's the sort of thing that a business owner should think... "Can I do that? Do I have that ability? Is that the best use of my time?" Absolutely, it's a better use of my time to really make sure that the marketing methods are performing the way that they're supposed to and then talk to the people as they come in from those Ad Words.

We use a combination of many things with Facebook. We also use many other plugins and programs. With our website we use Lead Pages, Optimize Press and other methods and programs that enable us to simplify and automate. Take a look at some of the ways to automate and start to use some of the programs you can integrate together.

Fitting The Pieces Together

We have a whole process we go through with each customer. We have it set up so that if they respond at specific points then the rest of the process doesn't trigger. Instead, it falls into a different part of the process. We use direct mail and along with it we use a program called Infusionsoft. We have all of our contacts in Infusionsoft and we know that we've sent them a direct mail. With direct mail we use both postcards and letters. We have sent out thousands' every month to different people that we're targeting, in different companies, to different individuals. Then depending on what is in the specific direct mail piece, we determine what out next steps will be. Many times we'll be sending email, making a phone call or both. Sometimes there's a fax involved.

I can give you an example for a specific training we delivered. We mailed a postcard, we faxed all of the companies and then we made a phone call. We touched them in a few different ways, and we know that it's working. For instance we had a call from someone to inquire about the training, and we asked them "How did you find out about it?" They received a fax. The offline or the old school marketing does work, but it has to be used in combination with other methods. I think of it as the circus plate spinner. He has to get one plate up and spinning and then he'll go and grab another plate and spin another one. But he has to kind of touch the first one every once in a while to keep it spinning. Then he goes and gets another and now he has three spinning. So that's kind of what the marketing is, you get one up and running and spinning and you just need to touch it every once in a while to keep it spinning and it kind of goes on its own. After a while you have six or seven or ten plates and that's when you really see the "wow this is something awesome" with your marketing. You soon have multiple methods in place and they're running automatically. So automatically that you can have somebody else running you're marketing for you. Just like our Facebook marketing, it's running automatically.

The Tools

A common tool we use and rely on is Hootsuite. It's a platform where you can schedule your social media posts. It means that you don't necessarily have to be tied to your Twitter or your Facebook accounts or any of your accounts because you can schedule posts to be posted later. At first I felt like that's not really authentic if I do that. Yet how it helps is amazing, it allows me to be there when my potential clients are using the various social media platforms. Some people are on Facebook or any other social marketing platforms in the morning and others are on in the afternoon, and others are on in the evening, but I can't be everywhere at all times. So the scheduling of the posts really allows me to connect and I can just go in and check to see who has replied to the post. It's not that I have to physically go and post it. I can just go check it and reply to some of the ones that are there.

Other things are within InfusionSoft. There are automation tools and tracking capabilities. I always encourage everyone to make sure that they look at Google Analytics to track marketing. We've used programs like Splash Post to help track the effectiveness of our post, to get people to sign up for our mailing list and say yes, raise their hand to say I want more information.

We've also had sales through our Facebook ads. We do different things in different areas to make sure things are as automated as possible and when we're helping companies, we're looking for those ways to automate their business processes.

Sometimes we suggest automation tools like Microsoft Database that they create or we help them to create. Remember we help companies with the strategy but we also do the implementation. If they don't have somebody that knows Microsoft Access, we might be the one to do that for them, to set it up for them so that it doesn't require anybody or it just requires that little bit of a spin on the plate to keep it running rather than a lot of effort all the time.

One of the most important things we use to simplify or automate social marketing is just having someone else do it. We have a great team. I get a lot of invitations on LinkedIn and someone on our team goes in there routinely and connects with the people for me or on my behalf, or accepts their invitation. A lot of times people reach out because they want to have a chat with me. So I have them set up a time to talk to me and we have a great connection. When you're working with clients just make sure that you're always giving them examples of your work and what it does for them because that's really what connects to them. Otherwise you become like I said earlier with the marketing, you become that company that says, "look at me, I'm a great company, you should do business with us. "You have to ensure that you're connecting with your ideal client.

The Programs

We're creating a program, a yearlong program and it's going to continually be added to so it will become a two-year program. Right now it's a one-year program, every month you'll get training in different areas and one on one time with me. The reason we did that is when we help businesses to grow we're really looking to help people to become more relaxed, to give them their life back, to grow their business and yet not overwhelm them. We have a quiz to start the process to see if you relaxed or are you to the max? Many business owners who come to us are to the max or they're well on their way to the max and they don't want to go there. The quick two-minute quiz will tell you where you're at, and we'll suggest some alternatives for you.

It has been a real eye opener for some of our clients to really take a look. Clients went from... "Wow I didn't think that I was, but you're right I am stressed" and other people know they're stressed and to the max but don't know what to do to get out of overwhelm. There are solutions out there; there are companies like us. I know some people, including locally who are closing their business. I just find it so sad because when I talk them, they've made the decision to close the business and they're already in that process. Once I talk to them they often wish they had known about our company even three months ago or six months ago because they wouldn't have to be closing their business if they had known there was some help out there.

We're really trying to get the word out internationally... Canada, United States, New Zealand, UK, we have clients globally. There are so many people that need the help. We're working with some large organizations to get the word out there, that there are companies like us who are out there to help, and that we are not just another consulting firm. We are Business Solutions Experts who help companies with growth. There are people/companies who give you a plan, you set it on the shelf and nothing ever happens. It becomes the worst investment you ever made.

Yes it costs money to work with us but we're different. We help you with implementation too. Even if we're not helping with the implementation, we continue to chat with you to see how's it going. We give you suggestions for tweaks and changes. We tell you, "No, don't do that, don't go down that path. Go down this path instead." We have clients who used to obtain $500 or $1000 clients and now they're getting $14,000 and $20,000 clients.

It comes back to... "You don't have to do it on your own". Yes, it is an investment to get the help, but its well worth it. People tell me... "You know what? I've done the research I can find the answers." Actually what our clients find is the more you read, the more you research, the more confused you become.

It's worthwhile to pay someone to help you to wade through all of that research that's out there, whether you actually do the research or not. We shortcut it for you, and that's why when we say we're helping people, we are the coach, consultant and mentor.

We're a coach, we'll pull the information from you when that's appropriate but other times you need the consultant. The consultant is the one who says, "Okay this is the way that you need to do it, this is what works". But other times you need the mentor, and the mentor is the person who holds you by the hand and says here let's get this done together.

So it's not that we necessarily do it for you. But many times it is done together. You're not alone and you don't have to wonder, "how am I going to find this?" "Is this even available?" "I don't even know anything about it." "Maybe I'm in the wrong business because I don't understand that."

No, you're not in the wrong business you just need some help. Reach out to us, if we're not the right fit for you we'll certainly tell you that and we'll also recommend somebody who can be a help or at least where to find the help that you need. We realise that not everybody is ready to work with us but most times we can provide some sort of guidance or help even if it is about how to do things in a certain way, a certain way to streamline something. It can be little tweaks but those little tweaks make the big difference.

THE UNIQUE TRANSFORMATION

Listen to our 13 experts as they reveal to you the unique transformation each one of them went through to get success in their business

www.crackingtheclientattractioncode.com

Program Your Inner Wealthy Woman to Create Consistent Income Online: Learn the Hottest Secrets in Building An Online Empire and Living the Life You Love

BY HEATHER PICKEN

CEO of Heather Picken Consulting International
Rule Breaker, Money Maker
Money Mastery Business Coach, Bestselling author

Creativity is God's gift to you. What you do with it is your gift to God.
— Bob Moawad

Secret 1:

Thinking from the End Result

My journey in creating my online empire, started with creating a product that product today. It's called **"The 6 week Fat-Burning and Mind Empowering System"**. Back when I had my own personal training business, it really inspired me to think outside the box. I was excited to realized how I could reach hundreds and thousands of people online, particularly women, with my system. I first started in a small office that I shared with a doctor. I had small workshops of women who I led through my 6-week program. The results were fantastic. The women were excited with their result and this triggered a light bulb moment for me. I knew I had I could make money online by sharing my expertise. I was excited to see this vision through.

However, I had one problem. I didn't know how to take my expertise and create a system where I could package and sell it online. I spent many months researching and buying different courses, and it felt overwhelming. Nevertheless, I didn't give up—that was the key and as a result, I made my very first sale for this product for $97. I was constantly changing the price to see what the sweet spot was. After selling my first program online, the question that popped in my mind was 'Oh my God, if I can sell one, how many more can I sell?'

Light Bulb Moment

Let's do the math...people buy my product at $97 with a push of a button. I was charging—$50 for an hour for my personal training. From there I designed a physical version of the system and doubled the price. How cool was that? My entrepreneurial mind was on fire!

"Envision the END RESULT of what you desire"

With the digital product, there was nothing that I had to do, except **receive the money in my bank account.** Can you imagine going from trading your time for dollars, to making money online where you could be out shopping, spending time with your kids, working out, and there is money waiting in your bank account? Pretty cool! I really got excited and motivated to figure out how to get my products out to women world-wide. I have to tell you that I wasn't the best marketer but I followed the strategies that I learned, I invested in myself and I didn't give up. I loved the idea of living anywhere I wanted. I was hooked in building my online empire. This motivated me further.

I didn't know how it would work either..I didn't have all the steps in my mind. However, I was holding on to the end result. **The key here is, you have to think from the end result.** If you think 'how can I do this?' or 'how is this possible?' Such questions start to take you away from your desires and that's where most people give up. It can be really overwhelming, especially building your online empire and not knowing what to do, but you don't want to give up when things get tough. You don't want to give up just because something doesn't work out e.g -you created a product and it doesn't sell, so what go back to the drawing board! You have to be true to your vision.

I wear this ring around my finger and it says **'Be True to Your Dreams'.** It is a constant reminder of the journey that I started and where I am today. It really gets me excited and inspired to help other women that are going through the same thing. They love that idea of creating, giving back, taking their expertise, wisdom and creating a service or product so that other people can benefit from it. If you're scratching your head and you feel overwhelmed right now with all the freaking information that's out there, you are not alone. It feels 'noisy', and you just want to give up, right? Here's my gift to you, all you need to do is to think from the **end result**. What does that look like for you?

The how's take care of themselves, I promise you.

Secret #2

Leading and Launching: How I Left My Personal Training Business and Created $40,000 in 6 Weeks

I mentioned earlier that I hired a mentor which was the best investment ever, because I really didn't know what I was doing nor did I have any sales background. I had some online experience but I was pretty new. When I told myself that I no longer wanted to be in the personal training business, and that I really wanted to go all out in the online world, there was no looking back! Yep, it was scary. The biggest leap for me was launching my first program that generated **$40K in 6 weeks. The key was having a mentor show me exactly what to do.. step by step.** Laying out the plan is really critical to your online success. However, the biggest thing that catapulted me was that I was constantly working on my mindset. I kept questioning myself, "Can I really do this? Who am I to **fill in the blank?** What kind of credibility do I have?" Sometimes I felt like giving up and abandoning the idea altogether but my coach kept encouraging me. "You can totally do this! You've got a gift to offer people", she would say. I remember feeling a switch in my brain of seeing my success and from then on I just told myself that there is no room for failure, that failure is not an option. I want you to tell yourself that, "There's no room for failure. Failure is not an option. If I stay true to my mission, purpose and vision, and if I play big, then I have to create success!" (Write this on a post it and really believe in these words)

"You've got to *think* differently, you have to *act* differently"

The biggest secret, was making the decision to be committed to my success. I knew I couldn't do it alone, I knew I needed a plan and I was also determined to reap, my investment that I was making. Therefore, you should not let yourself be discouraged by such thoughts like, "Oh, what if I invest in this program or work with this coach and I fail?" Your mind will dictate what happens to your money, so if you get it into your head and you tell yourself that story, you'll be stuck. You really need to stop saying that because it is not going to empower you in any way. Whether you're launching a new product or you're completely transitioning into this new space of being in the online world, **you've got to think differently, you have to act differently.**

I know so many people who come to me and they say, "Well Heather, I've invested so much money in all of these other programs. I don't know if I could spend any more money. I don't know if it's going to work." And I tell them the same thing, "So did I". I invested a lot of money. But the difference for me was that I was committed to my success. The question that you should ask yourself is, "How committed am I?" Do you want to be like everyone else that slowly tries to figure it out and maybe gets a little headway but not really into the bigger game that you want to play? Or do you want to be fearless, and tell yourself, *"You know what, I only have one life to live, I might as well just go for it. I'm going to let go of the fear. I am going to step into faith; I am going to move forward every single day. I'm going to do something that's going to rock. I'm going to take action. I'm doing something to change my mind and I'm going to get the support that I need, because I know I can't do it alone".* This is the kind of conversation that you need to have with yourself. I always tell people, 'Hey, I am not here to drag anyone along, I'm here to co-create this vision with you, become a partner, but only if you're willing to say yes to the journey, only if you're willing to move forward no matter what."

"You will generate hundreds and thousands of dollars very quickly if you take massive action"

Are there going to be little bumps and challenges on the the path to building your online empire? Absolutely. But the great thing is, if you realize this ahead of time, and if you understand that you have to tweak things as you go, you'll get to your goal. You'll have your first sale. You'll generate hundreds and thousands of dollars very quickly if you take massive action. If you immerse yourself into this launch, if you immerse yourself into creating an amazing vision for your online empire and realize you are here to help people with your services and products, I guarantee you, you will leave this world a better place, because after all, isn't that what it's all about

Secret #3:

Building an online empire to go

cha-ching, bling, and feeling freaking awesome

In order to build an online empire to make money and create the lifestyle that you deserve. You have to be strategic and create a plan, get clear on who your ideal client is, and the kind of products and services that you want to create. If you could close your eyes and just imagine what that might look like or how you would want it to be, this vision should be the fuel to get you motivated. In creating your products and programs, you need to think about some of the biggest problems that people have. The Imagine if you provided a solution, a product or service that fulfilled that need. How would that make you feel?

"People will pay you money if you can solve their problems"

The biggest secret when you're starting out or even when you have momentum in your online business is to redefine and tweak whom you're working with. Don't be so general; go ahead and dial it in. When I work with clients I help the to get clear around their niche. Remember to ask yourself these powerful questions:

What problems do people have?

Who do I really love working with?

From there, start creating your system based on these two questions. Many women make the mistake of trying to create online businesses based on what they think people want. You need to do your research first!

A CELEBRITY GUEST

An exclusive interview with Glenn Morshower, American Actor, best known for playing Secret Service Agent Aaron Pierce in 24. He shares the secrets of his success. And they are not what you think they are............http://crackingthecli-entattractioncode.com

---

CHAPTER EIGHT

Move Forward In A Creative Life In A Way That Is Productive, Fun and Profitable

BY SAMANTHA BENNETT
Creator The Organized Artist Company
The Organized Entrepreneur Company
Author, Teacher, Speaker
Bestselling author of, "Get It Done: From Procrastination to Creative Genius in 15 Minutes a Day" (New World Library)

Do whatever you know will help get the truth about what you do in front of the people who really need you. And if you don't know exactly what that is, then you'd either get some expert advice or you best start experimenting, honey!
- Samantha Bennett

I began to create The Organized Artist Company almost fifteen or twenty years ago with the "Get It Done" workshop. A workshop I devised mostly to deal with the issues that I was facing as an actor, writer and a teacher in Los Angeles. I just kept wondering... "how do you know what to do, how do you know how to move forward, how to start anything, maybe should you do a one person show, should you make a little film, should you be in a play, should you go on more auditions, should you buy a billboard on Sunset...who knows?"

That's how I started. It's hard to stay motivated when there's no quarterly review on how your novel is going. I knew I was creative and I've always been pretty good at getting things done. So I just started to look at that process and think, "How do you decide what the right step is?" and, "How do you stay motivated when you get discouraged? How do you move forward in a creative life in a way that is productive, fun and profitable?"

I showed this material to friends and other actors and word sort of started to get around, and it was always just one of a lot of projects and gigs and part time jobs. I was the girl of a hundred and seventeen part time jobs.

Then in 2009 all of a sudden my schedule emptied. All of a sudden a couple of things I was working on came to their natural conclusion, some stuff I thought I had lined up fell through and I had this big hole in my schedule. I thought, "Oh, great, now I've got to get another gig." Then I wondered if I could do the Organized Artist Company full time and then I thought, "I'd better get some business cards..."

So in pure ignorance, knowing nothing about business, nothing about marketing, nothing about computers, nothing about email marketing, nothing about anything, I started the Organized Artist Company and began teaching on line. And it's been incredible, I've doubled and tripled my revenue every year I've been in business. And you know, it's a delight. I mean, I have the best job I the world!

The Unique Transformation

One of the distinguishing factors about what I do is there's a lot of exercises and a lot of work sheets. It's not like I've got some incredible system and everybody should do things my way. That doesn't work for creative people.

What I do have is an incredible system that lets you figure out what your incredible system is. Jennifer Lopez's career works for Jennifer Lopez because she's Jennifer Lopez. Richard Branson's career has worked for Richard Branson because he's Richard Branson. People need to be able to have their life and work be an expression of the truth of who they are, and by definition, that can't be like anybody else. So that's really what my business is: helping people take a good hard look at their own creative process and then 'mine' that for the desire, energy and the decisions that are really going to work for them.

One of the things that happened in my career is that very early on in my business, I got Infusionsoft. Way before I really warranted it. I mean, I had a miniscule list. Infusionsoft is a sales and marketing software that allows Customer Relationship Management (CRM). It's like having email, Constant Contact, or Mail Chimp. It is like having a BIG rolodex, it's having everybody in your system and it allows you to tag people. It lets you know if people are interested in this, or they've clicked on that, or they've opened this, or they want more of that. Then it also has an e-commerce section so you can process orders. It's this big bear of a system, but I got it very early on because I knew that's where my business was going, I knew that's what I wanted and where I wanted to end up. I figured start with the best, don't play around. I've since become an Infusionsoft Certified Consultant.

But that first year I started using it was a big investment for me and I had no budget. So I needed it to pay for it before the American Express bill came. It really lit a fire under me. One of the things Infusionsoft can do is sending out automated emails. If somebody opts into my list, they go TheOrganizedArtistCompany.com and if they opt in for my latest free webinar they'll get a series of emails. The first bunch of them is... poems. They're sort of sweet and funny, there's one called 'Ode to the Overwhelmed'. The other one is 'In Praise of the Capable' and there's one for the grouchy and one for the over sensitive. They're very sweet, funny and 'forwardable'. I get a lot of people writing me back saying, "Oh, my gosh! I had to send that to my mom!" or, "Oh, my gosh, I had to send that to my sister."

I applied and was selected to be an Ultimate Marketer Finalist at Infusioncom that year for Infusionsoft. I was honoured for my marketing. I won a prize for my marketing. What I love about this is there is no business book in the world that says here's what you do: write a bunch of poems. This is not a standard tip. But because of who I am and because of who my people are, it really works for me. It allows me to scratch my writing itch, share my writing with the world. It also allows my people to really get to know me and who I am, my perspective and they feel like I know them. You know, by the time people get three or four of these they're writing me back like I'm their long lost college girlfriend. It's amazing.

So I end up with a list that's not just a list, it's really a community, and people that I have a very deep relationship with. I don't really think of them as clients or prospects, I think of them as friends.

Business Creativity

I had no idea that having my own business would be by far the best art project ever. Not to mention the best tool for self-discovery ever. I mean if you ever wondered what your inner-demon stuff was, start a business. It really calls you to grow up in some very significant ways. I do think of my business as a big art project. Being an entrepreneur means I have all this freedom to design new programmes and think of fun ways to market them to be able to think of fun ways to communicate with people and to really talk to them. When you look at where marketing and business is these days, all anybody wants to talk about is authenticity, storytelling and being of service. Nobody knows more about that than artists. That's what we do best. Entrepreneurs may or may not be artistic, but by their very nature, they are creative. There may or may not be room for art in your business, but in my experience there's no such thing as things being too entertaining or too beautiful. So I don't care if it's your lunch room, or your newsletter or your speech to the partners or if you're writing a chemistry textbook -- you know everything is entertainment. Not everything has to be funny or light, some things are very serious, but they can still be a rich emotional, personal experience and you really want to look for the opportunities. Don't think of it as, "Oh, I've got to write another sales pitch." Think of it as, "How can I really share my excitement with the people who really are hungry for this work?" Think of your emails as invitations to a party.

I think it was Seth Godin who said, "*if you've ever solved a problem differently than anybody else ever solved that problem, congratulations you're a creative genius.*" I really believe that. I love it when people get all zingy and cultivate the zingy feeling. No matter what you do... whether you have a massage therapy business or a shop, make sure to bring your other passions into it. If you send out a monthly letter, include your recipe for lemon bars, let people know about your butterfly collection, tell them about your flower arranging, or your race car or what you thought about last night's football game or whatever it is that you're passionate about. Bring that together with your marketing messages because people run in tribes. People who like stuff like other stuff too. People who like the same things tend to run in packs.

For example when I buy Facebook ads I look for people who like Annie Lamott, the writer, who like Elvis Costello, who like watching, "Mad Men," because those are things I like, and I figure if I like it my people probably do, too. This is where the best clients and best client attraction comes in. You want to be talking to people who have the same value system that you do and who like the same stuff you like. So you may be a car mechanic, but if you're also macrobiotic, make that a part of your marketing.

Attracting Clients

I'm pretty active on my Facebook pages and I'm lucky, because, you know, creativity and Facebook go together, procrastination and Facebook go together. Like bread and butter. So it's a lot of creative people and a lot of people who are not looking beyond their creativity. That works pretty well for me. I do a lot of word of mouth advertising and I get a lot of referrals for people. I do some speaking engagements and I'm active in a number of groups. I'm kind of a community-minded person so I'll work that way too. My experience is that when you are putting out a clear, authentic, truthful message about who you are and what you do, you become like the whistle only dogs can hear. The people who vibe with you will find you, and more importantly the people who do not vibe with you will not find you. Nothing is more expensive than a bad client.

I hear other teachers and coaches complain about how it would be so great if it weren't for the clients. I love my people, I have confidence in them, they could come for the weekend -- they're just wonderful. I never worry about selling them or not selling them. It's the right time for people or it's not. I don't have a lot of anxiety about it and I don't feel the need to beat the drum really hard. I mean I only need so many clients, I can't work with everybody anyway, so I really focus on building the community, keeping people entertained and talking to them about the pain of procrastination and the joy of creative productivity and fun ways to stay in contact.

Affiliate marketing is a part of my business model -- but I don't have "affiliates," what I have are people I know, that I think are amazing and they're up to some really, really exciting stuff. And sometimes I'll promote for them and sometimes I don't and sometimes they promote for me and sometimes they don't. So, again, we're back to this world of friendship and relationship. That's the other way I build my list, but I don't affiliate with just anybody. I wouldn't use affiliate "swipe" copy because if I'm recommending somebody it's because I really believe in them and I want to talk about why. While I'm always very clear when something's an affiliate offer, I mean it's the law that you have to disclose when something is an affiliate offer, but I would never promote anything that I wouldn't promote anyway, whether I was getting compensated or not.

I love finding people who do complimentary work to me. Like, I'll often mail for Evolving Wisdom, they do 'a find your soulmate course,' that's called, Calling In the One. I'll do a lot for people, but I'm not going to help you find a boyfriend -- you know, that's just not really my thing. I'll leave that to someone else. I'm delighted to promote stuff like that to my list I think it's great. I don't do it very often so my clients are generally quite responsive and don't feel too heavily marketed to.

I feel like we're headed into a whole new kind of economy, a whole new world that's actually very feminine, very female in its approach. It is open handed and more interested in relationships than profit. Well, not disinterested in profit (baby needs new shoes!) but very collaborative, real and very generous.

The great thing is buyers are buyers, workshop takers are work-shop takers. The fact that they take a workshop with you makes it more likely that they'll take a workshop with me. In the same way, the fact that somebody shops at Nordstrom makes it *more* likely that they'll shop at Macy's. So, you know, there's no shortage in the world. There's no shortage of money, there's no shortage of clients. I'm happy to promote for people when I know and I dig what they're doing.

Bringing The Clients Onboard

When I'm doing one of my bigger workshops, I usually commu-nicate with the participants exclusively through email, I'll do pre-view call, and little samples. This year I've started making more videos, too, so I can communicate with people through video. One thing that has worked really well with my high end and some of my lower end programmes is... I ask people to fill out an applica-tion. Even if there's no way on God's green earth that they're ever going to take this course, I say, "Go ahead and fill out the applica-tion anyway, because the action of answering these questions can often be really illuminating."

This accomplishes a couple of things. First of all, it has me ask-ing questions right from the get go and teaching the way I teach. And the way I teach is... I ask questions that people have to go deep and answer them and figure them out for themselves. It sets up that dynamic right away. People who like that are into it, and peo-ple who don't like that or don't want to do that go away. It gives me a chance to get to where they're at and the action to be taken. The other thing that it sets up is helping them understand this is really their project. They are the ones who are going to have to do the work; I can't do the work for them. Signing up for my "Get It Done Workshop" is not going to magically get your novel written, you're going to have to do it.

The application is not very long, but there are some interesting, provocative questions in there about where they're at, where they want to go and what they think is stopping them from getting there. And they get an automated response. This I do through Infusionsoft. They get an automated response right away that says, "Thanks so much for applying we'll review your application and get back to you." A lot of people fill it out just for fun and they make it very clear that they're not really interested in taking the course, which is totally fine.

But if I get the sense that they are interested or right for it, then they get an email from my assistant saying, "Great! We're so glad you're interested, if you just filled it out for fun, then no harm no foul, ignore this, but if you think you might be interested, click the Time Trade link and book a time to talk to Sam. Then they make an appointment call me. Again, I want to put the onus on them to call me at the appointed time and then we just talk. I find out where they're at and what's on their mind and why they think I might be able to help them and I tell the little bit about the programme, and what my expectations for the programme are. If it's one of my really high end programmes and it's really expensive, I tell them a little bit about the programme and then I say, "Are you ready to talk about the money?" And they say, "Yes." And I say, "Are you sitting down? Do you have a pen?" And they go, "Oh...."

I want them to notice. I took my VIP clients for a two day retreat in LA recently and I told them this is part of the reason this course is so expensive is because I need to get your attention. We pay attention to the things we invest in and if you really want to see movement, it's going to take your attention, and one of the ways to get attention is to charge a lot, so that's what I did.

Things That Don't Work

I offered a course on copywriting with a friend of mine a few years ago and it was really interesting. The launch was great, the material was strong, the people were opening the emails and clicking and we had a couple of webinars to promote it and those were well attended but no one signed up for the course. I realised that probably the topic was a little advanced for my list. Copywriting is possibly the most important skill you need to have if you're going to do your own marketing, but it's a little abstract. Nobody wakes up in the morning thinking... "I need to be a better copywriter." They wake up in the morning thinking... "I need more clients."

While the people on my list enjoyed the concept and the initial material, it was still a little down the road for them. They felt they'd need the copywriting later. Copywriting was part of what they needed but it wasn't really marketing to the core concerns of my people. It was something I did when this friend of mine asked me to do it and it sounded like a blast. Luckily on the internet no one can hear you scream. So we were able to just sort of skate past it.

Lessons Learnt

I just created different kinds of courses. One of them is called 'Start Right Where You Are.' It's geared for people who want to be more creative but aren't sure how. It serves some of the more foundational concepts and a deeper internal work than I do in the 'Get It Done' workshop. My big take away was just to keep my attention focused on who my people are and what they really need right now rather than what I think they should want.

Finding Ideal Clients

I'm not worried about making mistakes. If you don't make mistakes, that means you're just doing the same thing you've always been doing which is itself a mistake. So, I'm not so worried about belly flopping.

I do this thing -- which I think is frankly brilliant and I started doing this at the very beginning -- inadvertently -- I didn't realise that I was doing this.

See, early in my business I would just have people call me, I didn't have many structures in place, and it was... "If you're interested in working with me just call me, and we'll do a little twenty minute intake evaluation session." I really recommend having a little questionnaire. It really puts people at ease. It takes a lot of the tension out of that first conversation and it sort of helps me get right to the bottom of where they're at. After the initial questions like... "How did you hear about me", I would ask them, "So, how are you when you think about this project that you're not moving forward on?" and, "How do you feel right now, and how would you like to feel?" I just kept track of those and the words and phrases that recurred. Those words and phrases are <u>still</u> on the front page of my website. When you go to 'TheOrganizedArtistCompany.com' you'll see them right in front. Procrastinate-y...frustrated...nose pressed up against the glass...overwhelmed...when is it going to be my turn...I have thirty seven project ideas and I don't know which one to start with...all that is there.

I just took everything they were telling me about how they were feeling and then put it right up the on the front page of my website. And I hear from people all the time ... "Oh my gosh! It's like you've been reading my diary, that's so me." I say: I know, you told me.

Now that I have some more systems in place, whenever I offer a free webinar, a free tele-class and people sign up, I ask for their first name and email. Then I usually put another question in there and it's, "So what are you procrastinating on?" or, "What's keeping you stuck?" or, "What's your project?"...etc. It has been fascinating. That's how I found out that an enormous percentage of my lists are writers. I created a series called '365 Reasons to Write'. It's a book, but it's also available as a free daily email.

The last webinar I did I asked people... "What do you think is keeping you stuck?" And they were so forthcoming...oh my fear of success, my fear of failure, my diverticulitis, my this, and lots of other things. I put them all into Wordle.com. Wordle makes word clouds, the more frequently a word appears the larger it is in the word cloud. I just took all those responses, I didn't edit them -- put them into Wordle and then got this word cloud and it was like boom, there's a graphic of your psychographic right there. I put it up on the sales page. So whatever they're feeling... overwhelmed, anxiety, fear of success, fear of failure....it is there in the word cloud, all this stuff right there in front of them.

When people are first looking at your website, they're not reading it, they're just *looking* at it. If they see something that reminds them of themselves then they will start to read. A graphic word cloud really captures their attention if it's right for them. If it's not right for them then it doesn't, which is just as important. 'TheOrganizedArtistCompany.com' is where all my great stuff is, my blog is there, my website is there, and a ton of free resources and free recordings. You're welcome to just hop on the list. Once you're on the list you'll get the poems and all kinds of fun stuff. I would love people to hop over and if nothing else be entertained and see if they can find stuff to help them.

The Best 'Marketing' Strategy

I think "marketing" is a terrible word. The entire marketing vocabulary is terrible, "drip sequences" and "lead magnets," it all sounds awful, I don't know why marketing has such a terrible vocabulary. There's nothing about the word 'marketing' that conveys the truth of what it really is. I always think of it as making friends with people you don't know are your friends yet. Just reach out and let people know about what you're doing, that you love it and if you can be of service to them. Think of it as a conversation and keep your eye on the conversation of marketing. Don't make it a one way conversation and don't be afraid to use your own voice, don't be afraid to really talk to people about where they're at. Learn from my mistake about the copywriting course: talk to them about their concerns not what you think they should be concerned about. Start to enjoy the rhythm of it, because there is a rhythm to marketing, there is a rhythm to attracting new clients and it's not something that you just do once and set and then it's done.

Sometimes I think entrepreneurs just wish that this whole "marketing" and "getting new clients" thing would just go away. A lot of times people think, 'can't someone else do this, can I hire a sales person, can't I hire a copywriter', of course you can and lots of people do, but I think when you do that you're cutting yourself off from the real life blood of your business. Put yourself really in deep communication with the people who are interested in what you do. I wouldn't deprive myself of that opportunity; I would really learn to love it. That's my advice... learn to love it.

My people write back to me and when other internet marketers hear the size of my list and how responsive it is, they freak out. But I hear from people all the time, my inbox is way too full. I get unsubscribes too, God bless the unsubscribes. I don't want to annoy anybody, if my stuff isn't working for you, go fly, be free people. Yes! It's really possible.

ON ATTRACTING CLIENTS

For more ideas and inspiration about attracting clients, dive deep into what each of our experts has to say http://crackingtheclientattractioncode.com

---

CHAPTER NINE

Do YOU Need To Build A List?

BY ERIKA KALMAR
Business Success Mentor
Founder of Get Ready To Coach
Host of the Giveaway For Coaches and the 14 Days To More Clients training

"Our greatest weakness lies in giving up. The most certain way to succeed is always to try one more time."

—*Thomas. E. Edison*

There are so many people who are going ahead with list building without being clear with the real reason behind that – why they want to do that at the end of the day.

They feel like... 'Oh, I'm hearing that this is what I need to do', so they are just doing it. They have to reconnect with the real reason and the real motivation if they really want to succeed in list building.

Not everyone needs a list. You certainly **don't need a list if you master two things**:

#1: If you are a master networker, meaning that you're really good at going out and looking for local clients, for instance going to local networking events and *pull leads* from there. Or if you're operating in a more global setting, then setting up global strategies for lead generation and implementing them on a *consistent* basis. This is one thing. If you are really mastering this, that's half of the success.

#2: Mastering enrolling clients from strategy sessions, from tele-classes etc. is the second thing you need, because it's not enough to generate lists, you also need to *convert* those leads into clients.

If someone has *both* these two skills (mastering networking AND mastering enrolling clients), then they don't need a big list because they can make a really great living on those things that they are doing already.

Most entrepreneurs don't own both these skills and that's when list building comes into the picture.

Building a big *responsive* community is a great way to **build a rock solid foundation** for your business.

Why? Because let's face it – the coaching market is **saturated** now. If you remember back, twenty years ago or so, there were only a handful of coaches out there on the market. Their job was quite easy because interested people contacted them to hire them and that was it!

I don't think *anyone* experiences scenarios like that nowadays. There is a huge supply of coaches and the market just doesn't work the same way anymore.

Just looking at the coaching school that I graduated from, there are eighty new coaches graduating each trimester – from my coaching school alone. That means that almost **three hundred new coaches** enter the marketplace every year, only ONE coaching school.

Multiply this number by one hundred or two hundred, I'm not sure how many coaching schools there are out there. Add to it the number of coaches who have not attended any coaching schools. I would say there are thousands of new coaches and other heart-based professionals entering the market every year.

With this huge market supply, isn't it normal that potential clients are getting cautious about choosing the right fit?

By building a big responsive community and keeping regular contact with them, staying in front of them, nurturing them, you give those people the opportunity to get to **know, like, and trust you**.

At the end of the day, they give you their email address and if you stay in front of them *on a regular basis*, they will want to take the next step with you, and again the next step, and again the next step.

If you have a 3,000-4,000 size list (and here I'm talking about a responsive and really *targeted* list), that could be **a solid base for a six figure income**.

That's how important a list is...

How to Build Your List (And How You Won't)

There are a trillion ways to build your list. In fact, each expert will give you a different strategy.

Funnily, if somebody had asked me this question three or four years ago, my answer would have been something **completely different than today**. Most probably I would have advised business owners to do article marketing and set up their irresistible free offer, get an opt-in box on their website, do social media etc.

You see, when I started with my business, I was all over the place, I must admit. I was so desperate to build my list! I wanted to be everywhere, so I did article marketing, I participated in 20-30 online forums, I was literally everywhere in the virtual space, in every relevant groups on Facebook and LinkedIn.

Now I have a different take on this.

What I realised over the time is that although these strategies are great and they work, **they take years to build a big enough list**.

Because with these strategies (whether with your website or article marketing) you're growing your list **adding ONE person at a time**.

Don't misunderstand me – I still have a website and I still do have a great free gift on it for people. But this strategy is **NOT fast enough**.

And that's how I turned to a faster-paced list building method...

Forging Strategic Partnerships – And Three Levels To Do That

Yes – forging strategic partnerships is the new currency!

There are **different levels** though of working with partners.

Level #1 for me is forging a partnership with **one specific partner at a time** – which is great because you have exposure in front of an additional audience.

The problem is – it is one single partner.

Of course, you can rinse and repeat this process. I know many coaches who interview an expert or get interviewed by an expert every month and that's a great way to *consistently* add people to your list.

Level #2 is when you are featured in the **expert panel of big virtual events**, high-quality telesummits or giveaway events.

Once you're sitting in the expert panel of a virtual event that is so much more powerful because you have a much **higher exposure**. You will be presented to the *joint community* of all the experts in the panel.

Another great thing about being part of such events is that they are *time limited*. My Giveaway For Coaches event for instance is 14 days. My 14 Days To Get Clients event took (guess what) 14 days!

It means that by being invited to virtual events, you can **explode your list in a very short time**.

Level #3, and this is for me the **highest impact list building strategy**, is when **YOU host an event**.

There are so many benefits of that!

Many people think that it's just about the list but it's much more than that because once you host your own event then it automatically positions you **as the go-to expert**.

You get tons of **visibility** because you are seen together with other big names that are in your event.

Not to mention the fact that by keeping contact with your event visitors you immediately increase the 'know-like-trust factor' with them, so it will be **easier for you to turn these hot leads into paying customers**.

Of course one of the biggest benefits of hosting your own event is that you will **build a much bigger list of targeted and interested prospects** than if you would be just an expert invited to someone else's event.

It is logical – if you are a guest expert, only those people will opt in to your gift who *at that moment* are interested in your topic. You can nurture them and upsell to them, but you will lose out on all other event visitors who DIDN'T leave their email address with you.

If you are the event host, every visitor needs to opt in to YOUR list. There is no way around that.

That's why it is so much more powerful to be an event host. You're literally multiplying your list building results.

Let me give you an example.

I've been hosting my Giveaway For Coaches event for the third year now. Typically I'm **increasing my list by 3,000 highly targeted prospects** every time I'm hosting it, all **in a timespan of only 14 days!**

That's huge! How does it compare to the 200 to 500 people who opt in with me when I'm a guest at others' event? Well, you tell me!

Telesummit or Giveaway Event?

I'm often asked the question: *"Shall I host a telesummit or a giveaway event – which one is best?"*

Everyone is different, so other things might work out for one person or the other. I've done both, but my giveaway event was my first virtual event so I consider it as my first baby.

Still I would like to give you a couple of hints in terms of the **pros and cons** for both.

I encourage you to choose based on which type of event works best in your case.

For example if you like interviewing, **if you like speaking**, if you're really buzzing on a live call, do a telesummit. It is the best option for you, it builds on your natural strength.

Many people ask for help from me who know that they 'should' do a virtual event but they **hate speaking**. What I reply is – either ask someone else to do the interviews for you or opt for a give-away event.

If you **don't like to be in the spotlight** or interview people, then a giveaway event is the perfect solution for you.

Another aspect – there is **NO live component** at a giveaway event.

Obviously there are many telesummits today that run with pre-recorded trainings. For example, my 14 Days To More Clients summit was just like that.

But the majority of telesummits have a live component (the interview itself or handling the chat box), which means that **technical glitches** can come up on the live call.

If you do a giveaway event, you **set up everything in advance**. There's no live component – you just set up the event opt-in page, you set up the gift page and you are ready to launch your event. When the event ends, you let people know on your opt-in page that doors are closed, and that's it!

There are three other things that I'd like you to consider as well.

There are **less giveaway events on the market than telesummits**. If you have difficulties in finding the competitive edge for your virtual event, then with your giveaway event you will **stand out more** than with a telesummit.

With a telesummit, you need a really great concept, a topic that people jump on. Because let's face it – people are NOT going to sign up for your event if you're just putting together a bunch of interviews without having a common theme or a good concept, **even if it's a free event.**

There are so many telesummits out there. If you are **unsure about your concept**, then you're better off with hosting a give-away event.

Also, you have to **think about your target market.** For example, typically in a telesummit people invite 12, 14 or 20 experts. That means **10-20 hours of recordings**! Look at your target market and establish if this is something that they would consider doing.

For example, if you are serving corporate executives, chances are they are NOT going to take the time to enrol in a telesummit and listen to 20 hours of recordings. This is typically a case when you would rather create a giveaway event – and the best is to put together one that offers quick resources. They will love that.

These are just a couple of things that you might want to consider when making your decision about the type of event you are going to host.

There is one final question that I'd like to answer for you. Oftentimes I hear this question: "Wait Erika, I know you can monetize on a telesummit, but **can you earn money with a giveaway event?**"

YES, YOU CAN!

You can monetize on your virtual event, whether it's a telesummit or a giveaway event.

The #1 Key to Hosting a Successful Giveaway Event

There are many keys, but if I had to choose only one, I would say without hesitation: the #1 success factor is your CONCEPT.

As I just mentioned it above, people are NOT signing up nowa-days for something just because it's free. There are so many free events and free resources available on internet that *people are getting very selective.*

Therefore you have to have a great concept.

That will do two things for you:

First, if you have a great concept for your giveaway event, it will be super easy for you to *attract visitors.*

There's nothing more sad than working a lot to put together an event where no one shows up.

If you have a good concept, then *masses of people* will flow to your event and people will *share* your event with their friends.

But it's not just about visitors – it's also about partners!

If you don't have a good concept, then it will be difficult for you to *enrol your partners to your vision.*

By developing the right concept you attract both visitors and partners.

Once you decided on your concept/topic, do a 360 degree evalua-tion of it to see if it's the **right fit for ALL parties** involved:

Is it a good fit for you? Meaning – does it fit in your overall service offering?

Is it relevant for you? This will be important so you can up-sell to one of your services.

Is it a good fit for your audience? You don't want to get hundreds of unsubscribes from your current prospects (unless you are re-branding and you don't need them anymore).

Is it a good fit for your partner – and their audience? Otherwise, your partners won't promote it for you!

If all these boxes are checked off, then you are ready to organize your event.

Traps to Avoid

I would like to mention the three biggest traps that event hosts fall into.

Mistake #1: Not shooting high enough

This is what I experience with most of the people who are coming to my Giveaway Event Secrets program. They say: "I'm just starting my business, *who am I to approach all those big gurus out there?*"

Instead, they approach their mastermind members who are at the same level in list building as them. They partner up with ten of these business owners who also have only thirty people on their list, including their Mom and their dog. And once the event ends, they will only have *a handful of new prospects* after all that great work!

Don't fall into this trap!

People tend to think that "**I can't ask all those big names to partner with me, provide a free gift and even promote this event for me.** That's a big favor to ask, isn't it?"

Change your perspective around this...

You're NOT asking for a favor.

Put this mentality aside.

You are offering something really, really valuable to your partners because **you're offering them exposure in front of a joint community** of 10, 15 or 20 other experts. It's a real win-win for both you and them.

That's the mindset that I'd like you to get into!

For my first Giveaway For Coaches event I invited some successful entrepreneurs that I really admired at the time when I started my business. I always thought they are big, unapproachable experts, but I thought – "Why not? *What's the worst thing that can happen?*"

That I get a "no"? And so what?

So I reached out to them and guess what – they said "yes"!

Can you imagine how euphoric I was? They were idols of mine and they want to participate in my event – and they are even going to promote my event to their whole list!

I would really like you to live this experience and this feeling...

Not shooting high is a big mistake, so go for people you admire, who are big authority on their marketplace and are likely to have a big, responsive community.

(Hint: And if you have a good concept, it will be easy to enroll them, remember?)

Mistake #2: Not stepping up as a pro

If you're hosting a virtual event, don't spare money on your virtual assistant or on creating a professional look.

You want a **professional** event opt-in page and you want to have professional emails queued up for your partners and visitors to go out before, during and after the event.

There is only ONE first impression and if your partners send thousands of great leads to your event page, you'd better make this first impression good, otherwise they are gone.

It's also about your partner's reputation. Don't disappoint them, have a professional appearance. *Hire a VA* (Virtual Assistant).

Here is a **bonus tip** for you: the best is if you hire a virtual assistant who has already experience in managing virtual events because you don't need to train them or explain them what you need. They will know exactly what to do – and they can generate additional ideas for your event promotion.

For example, for my VA it took 10 hours to set up everything. For $20 you can find a good VA. This investment is really nothing as opposed to the results that you are getting out of it. I rejected several partnership proposals just because that person had an opt-in page that felt too home-made. Don't make this mistake!

Mistake #3: Expecting partners to do ALL the promotion

The power of a giveaway event lies in the *joint promotion effort of all partners*. But this doesn't mean that you can sit back and relax while they do all the work!

You have to **lead by example** and motivate them so they promote your event as much as they can.

And in order to effectively promote your giveaway event that lasts such a short time, you have to put together a *Promo Plan* in advance.

Sit down and create a plan on where and how you will reach targeted prospects (involve your VA in the brainstorming).

Make your event a success story for your partners.

Earning Money From Your Event

The ultimate aim of hosting a telesummit or giveaway event is to get new prospects and **convert** them to clients so you earn money.

And if you have a good sales funnel in place, you WILL earn money with your event – long term.

It takes time to build the relationship with your leads, you have to stay in front of them, send them lots of great content before they will be ready to buy from you.

But there are couple of ways how you can **monetize on your event short term**, too:

One thing is charging **participation fee**. This is a standard practice with giveaway events.

I know that telesummit owners do NOT charge for experts to join. In giveaway events though it's a standard practice to charge a participation fee. It can be anything between $50 and $200 (and this can go up once your reputation as "the" giveaway event host is established).

If you are charging $100, and you have 20 guest experts, then it's already a good starting income for you that will **cover all your costs, including your virtual assistant** and much more than that!

That's one thing that you can do.

Another thing you can do is to **package** the event content and sell it like a telesummit package.

Many people think of selling a telesummit package once the event ends, but hardly anyone thinks of doing the same with a giveaway event!

One of my Giveaway Event Secrets program graduates did exactly this! She had the idea of creating a giveaway event offering

1-2 page quick resources. Then she had the idea to package these and sell them as a product once the event was over.

That's a second way how you can monetize on your giveaway event.

Then of course a third thing is to earn **affiliate commission** on your partner's up-sells. That's really good.

I highly encourage you to put in place an *affiliate link* for your partners because with that you can earn money from their sales coming from people that your event sent to them – and by tracking their link, you can *monitor their promo activity* as well. Two birds with the same stone...

Of course a fourth way to monetize on your event is to **up-sell** to one of your products or service. You can up-sell on the back of your giveaway event a low priced item, a $97 item for instance, or one of your group programs – something on the lower investment scale.

AND something that is a *natural next step* for your event visitors to take with you. (You cannot put together an event offering business building resources and then invite people to purchase a dating course!)

So these are just some of the ways how you can monetize on your event short term.

Final Tips

I said this already but I'd like to highlight this again since it's so important:

Hire a virtual assistant; don't try to spare money on the expense of professionalism and risking burn out. Let the professionals put this together for you. You don't want to get lost in the technical details of how to connect your affiliate program with your shopping cart etc.

Do the strategic work and delegate the rest. I gave you above some ways how you can even recoup your investment with your event, so there's really no reason for you to be a DIY-er. This is what some of my Giveaway Event Secrets program graduates just did: they took my course, put together their unique event concept and partner list and sent the rest to their VA.

The other thing is... 'just do it'.

Don't procrastinate, just do it.

I will tell you why:

Many people tell me *"Erika, this is a brilliant list building tool – I will host my event once my business foundations are in place".*

Don't do that!

Building your list is YOUR business foundation! In fact, that's your second step, right after clarifying your niche.

You can spend time and money on polishing your perfect website and creating great products but – you need a list so people go to your perfect website and purchase your great product!

And this is what hosting your event can do for you...

Keep in mind that while a giveaway event lasts about 14 days, you need to give a **3 months' lead time** for your partners so they can fit into their promo calendar.

So if you procrastinate until you *desperately* need a list, it will be already far too late for you. You want to get started with this as soon as possible.

The best way to stop procrastinating is that you take your calendar (do it right now!), look at 2-3 months from now, and pick a date now. Check if there is no major holiday in between or something that keeps your ideal clients away from your event and book it in your calendar.

And then announce it! Tell it to the whole world. Tell it to your mastermind peers, your coach, your friends, your spouse, your grandma, your clients, so that you hold yourself accountable and then you must really do that.

That's a great thing because you will be really on your way to great list building success and if you still feel like procrastinating, then I am willing to jump on a quick call with you. I want to get you unstuck on this and move you past your fears.

I experienced firsthand the benefits of building a big list (approaching 10,000 now), gaining visibility, be mentioned together with big industry leaders, getting tons of rave emails from event visitors and finally, the financial freedom that all this can bring.

Is it scary? It is all normal. It's part of the process.

You are growing and for this you need to step out of your comfort zone.

If it gets too scary, reconnect with your ultimate why and visualize your event's success.

And ask yourself the question – **"What's the worst thing that can happen?"**

INSPIRING CLIENTS TO SAY "YES"

You'll get great ideas that you can model when you visit
http://crackingtheclientattractioncode.com

CHAPTER TEN

Your Potential Client's First Impression, Your Website, Ensure It's a Good One

By Frank Deardurff
Web Strategist
CEO of Orange Pixel, Inc.
President of That One Corporation
Author, Artist

"You never get a second chance to make a first impression".
—Andrew Grant

The Calling...

I think it was more by chance. I had a love for graphics. It was my passion and it always has been as far back as I can remember. I've always been doodling on something or drawing or sketching or whatever. When I got out of high school I wasn't exactly sure what I wanted to do. I met with the college counsellors and they got me introduced into AutoCad, which is a form of drafting. It was about designing houses or buildings or sewers, infrastructures and things of that sort. I kind of liked that a little bit because it was using my technical art abilities, which I have a high eye for detail when I'm doing graphics.

As I moved on, I actually did work in that field for a bit but I ended up going back to college a second time to update the Auto-Cad that was outdated (the newer versions and things like that). I got more involved into graphics and of course with that being my passion I had some 3D artwork that I do. I like doing wallpapers for the back of your computer screen. I've done some print work and painting and things like that but I was doing some of these 3D modelling and things like that. I was trying to figure out a way that I could share them.

Of course back then when I first started doing that we didn't have the technology that we do now. We didn't have easy access to create a webpage. It was done through Geocities or AOL Member's pages and things like that. I started actually with an AOL member's page before you could easily buy domains and put up things. Of course some of the bigger search engines like Google weren't around so you just kind of had to trial and error and try to figure it out yourself.

That's actually how I got bit by the web bug. I started reading, and learning, and following, I had to do everything as I said the hard way. I had to look at the code and see how different people did things. There were other people at that time that started doing things and I started following people then. I just picked it up as a knack. I started with the 3D wallpaper images that I had, I'm also a genealogist so I liked looking up that type of thing. I tried to figure out ways that I could list the things that I found or things that I'm looking for. With the resources that I found I actually put up my first website with both of those hobbies.

A friend of mine that I worked with at that time, Bret Ridgway, you may know him over at Speaker Fulfillment Services. We were working at a sister company together at the time. I was doing technical illustrations and he was involved in finance and marketing for that company. He'd seen some of the work that I was doing and they were looking at getting on the website. I started helping them with their website. Some of the marketers that he was working with, especially people like Alex Mandossian, had seen some of the work that I did. One thing led to another and that's pretty much how I got to where I am.

I enjoy being able to do what I love and being able to travel. With the Internet and the things that we do, we're able to work anywhere. Next week I'll be at a live event and I can just pack up my laptop and I can work in the evenings or work during sessions or whatever. To me, it doesn't seem like work because I'm enjoying it but I can do it anywhere. It's great.

The Unique Transformation

I offer a few different resources, so I'll just list a couple of them. The service that I provide mostly is being a direct response Webmaster. I've taken some of the techniques that have been around for probably centuries now. Direct response mail has been around for a long time. People would get in the mail, letters that tried to sell a product or maybe newspaper articles or things like that.

They would use newspaper ads to create a direct action from either the letter. Letters that said... "if you act right now..." or "try a sixty day subscription..." Those were done before the cable market or even websites were available. I've just applied those strategies to the web.

We look at the web as being just another form of media. Some people originally looked at it as being some sort of digital Amway type of scenario where everybody was trying to have multi-level marketing schemes and things. It's just more or less a different media. It is about applying those strategies to the web so that people can put up a sales letter online or have a nice looking page and make sure that you use those interactions to create a direct response.

The other thing that I do that is a little bit different is I do trainings. I show people how they can better improve their website and many times I show them how they can do it themselves. Obviously with the people that I work with I'm limited in the time that I'm able to actually do things for people and it frustrates me when I see people that have no direction, they don't know what to do.

They say, okay somebody said I need to do this, but how do I get it done or who do I get to do it? Then they try to find the right person, as you know good web people are hard to find because they're usually busy and it takes way longer. What I try to do is I try to teach people that it isn't difficult. A lot of people are afraid of technology but it's not so much the technology. They've just never been shown how to do it. It's generally pretty easy and inexpensive.

On Attracting Clients

Social media is very big these days as is attending live events. There's a lot of streaming events going on right now and that's great if you can't travel. Maybe it's just not in your budget. When you look at the possibility of a live event, you think 'oh there's a lot of expense, there's travel, I've got to get there,' but it's way more than just the event.

I've made so many joint venture partners by attending live events. I go and pass out my business cards. You have a thirty second elevator speech that you rehearse and get ready so that when somebody says what do you do, you're ready to go. You can tell them what you do.

A lot of times you actually make quite a few sales yourself of your products, or coaching, or your book, or whatever. You start your funnel from these live events because it's easier to connect with people one on one live than it is digitally. Attending live events is a good way to attract more clients.

One of the main reasons I created my book 'The 50 Biggest Website Mistakes' was to tell people about some of these mistakes and how to fix them. But it also gets them interested in the courses and the services that I offer.

It's kind of like a bigger business card if you look at it that way. I recently started a podcast and in some parts I'm talking about a chapter or a section of my book. I'm talking about one of the 50 Biggest Website Mistakes. Of course I said if you like this mistake you can get the book and get all Fifty at once instead of waiting fifty weeks or however long I can stretch it out. I give business tips and resources and things like that as well on the podcast.

Doing interviews is a good way to attract more clients because people get to know who you are and get to see your personality a little bit more. I did a speaking event in front of about four hundred people for a homeschool group back in the August. You make all those connections. You make yourself available. You don't just go and speak, walk off and then hide in your hotel room. I think it's important to make yourself available where you stay in the room yourself. You stay in the hallways and stand around and talk and give people ideas.

Then they say hey, this guy was one of the speakers but yet he's approachable. He's somebody I can reach and connect with. If you have coaching, or if you have a product or service you want to be reachable. You want them to think that they can reach out to and make a connection. I think those are great ways to build and attract new clients.

Little Tweaks That Make a Big Difference

A few of the things that people need to think about are things we don't pay attention to. Things that we take for granted but it's actually psychological. You think about the colour of your website... the background colour, the foreground colour, the header. You have to think of what's best for your market. You can't just go with your favourite colour. I've tried that... my favourite colour is orange but if you go to any of my websites I've kind of switched that and used it more as an accent colour instead of being a background colour or anything like that.

You have to be careful because if it's an off-putting colour to some people, it may be your favorite color and the best colour in the world, but if it's off-putting to them, they may not stay on that website very long. It may distract them. It's proven that certain colours work in different markets.

So if you used a lot of red on a site that you're trying to build trust, you're not going to do it because it creates a different type of emotion. Red actually works better on food sites as you've probably noticed McDonald's and Pizza Hut. A lot of those food sites have red in them. Where if you visit, say a financial site or somebody that's wanting to build trust, there are more shades of blue, blue-grey, and steel blues, and things like that. If you look again at medical sites or health sites, a lot of those tend to be blue or even more so green than anything. It's a good idea to do a little bit of research and find what colours work. As you may hear me say many times, test everything. Test the background colours. Test the header colours, even test the font colours.

Another thing would be your headline. That's the first thing that somebody reads when they come to your website. You need to make sure it answers the question why am I here? I stumbled on this because I'm not a copywriter or I'm too close to the project on my own products. A good friend of mine, Lori Morgan-Ferrero, she's a copywriter, tells me it's a good idea to keep in mind that when you're writing a headline for your copy, it is the selling point and gets them to read the rest of your sales page. She recommends writing a hundred different headlines and to modify them a little bit each time. By the time you get to a hundred, you will end up coming out with a better headline.

I know that sounds like a lot of work and I don't think I've ever reached a hundred before I had to say okay this one works. Then I start testing, or tweaking, or changing a word. I'll put it up, on the social media, which makes it so much easier. I'll pick the top three that I like or the top five that I'm interested in trying and I'll post it on Facebook and say which of these most appeal to you? Or I'll post it to a mastermind group that I'm in and find out which appealed to them. Many times what I thought would be the winner is usually the loser or not even close. They'll modify and give me better options. That makes a big difference.

Professionalism Matters

Some of the things that people don't think about on their websites are also things that attract clients. With so many possible scams out there, I think we need to make sure that our site actually looks like a professional site or a business website instead of one that the next door neighbour's kid did in the garage scenario.

It actually, not only increases sales and conversions it also gets a lot of people come to our website. When you first start, you only have a matter of seconds to make an impression whether they're going to click and move on or read a little bit more and a little bit more. We want to try to increase that time from a couple of seconds to ten, fifteen, whatever time it takes them to buy. So we need to make sure we have things like a logo on our website instead of just a headline.

There are various websites out there that are just a headline on a sales page, and it might work for a some but if you're trying to attract clients, you're trying to build a repertoire with them, you're trying to have a relationship with them, you need to have consistency with logo and your colour and your branding and things of that sort.

The search engines favour that heavily by having a logo in your site and having your legal disclaimers in your footer. I see a lot of sites that do not have that. That's one of the things I overlook when trying to throw a site up quickly. I have to go back and add a footer and terms of service. That shows that your site is actually a business website or you're actually a legitimate company. Those are a few more things that I think that people need to think about on the website.

Google experts tell me that they actually look for things like that. They look for a logo. They look for the legal disclaimers. They look to make sure you have a headline that's marked with H1 tags, which is HTML and I won't get techie here but H1 and H2 tags and things of that sort. They actually look for that type of thing on the website. It does make a difference whether we think it does or not.

Inspiring the Client to Say 'Yes'

I think the biggest thing is to be honest. Be who you say you are and stick with it. I think you see a lot of flip-flopping and things of that sort. Don't sound hype-y. I strongly believe that if it sounds too good be true, then it generally is. I've seen people put on their site... 'if you use my product in the next thirty minutes you could earn up to $50,000'. That's surely going to get you in trouble with the FTC or whatever authorities are in your country or state. You need to be careful about financial statements such as that.

But I think you need to be honest. You need to build a relationship. If you're selling a more expensive product or service, you need to carefully think about it. An opt-in is always good. Earlier it was called a name page or a squeeze page or an opt-in page and you'd get there before you'd even get to the sales letter. We've kind of moved away from that for a little bit and I see sites going back to that now.

I always had better conversion when I did have an opt-in of some sort up. An opt-in is just a box off to the right always on the right because your scrollbar and things like that are on the right and your mouse is generally on the right side. Webpage studies have shown if you have it on the right there's more chance that they're going to see it. There's more chance that they're going to click on it to create a better action.

But at the opt-in, you want to give them a free report or a free trial or maybe if you have a CD or music or some type of audio, give them a free clip. Give them maybe a fifteen to thirty minute video of your training or a sample of your training. If they give you their name and email, you're rewarding them by doing so.

But don't just stop there. I see a lot of people will stop at that point. So if you're selling a coaching program that may cost $2,000 that's almost like asking for marriage on your first date. You want to romance them. You want to court them into buying your more expensive product. And you do that by creating an auto-responder series. After they opt-in that first time, you create a series of emails that you load into your auto-responder service, which is a subscription service that you buy and it'll end up paying for itself pretty quickly.

You put in a day one message, and a day three message, a day five message, a day seven, and it goes as long as it takes. Generally, it could be twenty one days. It could be thirty days. It could be one message a day for the next week, or it could be one message a week for the next year. Whatever works best for you. Of course, there are ways that once they buy you can take them out of that series and then follow up with that. But the types of messages that you might want to use in that opt-in series would be if you're selling a book, you could say or if you're doing like a book that has training in it or something like that. You could say did you see on page five of your free chapter that we talk about this strategy? Give them a link to go back and maybe you had a PDF on there or whatever. You tell them a little bit about that strategy and then they'll go back and read it. You helped them consume the sample that you've given them.

Then you wait a few days and you say, did you see in page seven we talk about this? Or if you had a video you could say, did you see in minute five of the video we talked about this strategy? You want to make sure that they consume it because if they get something from you and they don't consume it then they're going to think less of you because that wasn't a very good product. I didn't learn anything from it. Well, they never listened to it. They never read it.

Helping them consume it, they're going to consume it and they're going to find out hey I did learn something from this, and then they're going to eventually buy your product, which is the end goal that we want too.

By creating that courtship, or creating that relationship with them, you're creating a long-term relationship. If you get them to buy the first product, there are better chances of them buying a second or third. They become a long-term customer with you. If you create a courtship with them you have a better chance of getting them saying yes many more times rather than just once.

Learning From Failures

One of my favorite quotes is "A mistake is truly a mistake if you learn nothing from it." I think, as I said many times, testing is very important. If you visit any of my websites once you may not see the same headline when you go back a different time because you're always increasing conversions. One of the things that doesn't work is a stale website. Things that don't change. Even if it is working, you may change it and find out that your conversions are even better. A stale website is something that doesn't work. It's also been proven that a stale website doesn't have any change to it. When the search engines notice it doesn't change you lose spots in the search engine. You want to change it up a little bit or add more to it. That's why maybe having a blog attached to a sales page where you're blogging about the product increases conversion because the site's changing. Even though it's on a blog page, it's still part of the site. That shows that the sites changed or something's changed on this website and the search engines come back and keep you relevant. A stale website doesn't work.

You want to make sure you don't give the reader too much to read. I'm not saying that you shouldn't have a lot of content. You shouldn't have paragraphs that are more than four or five sentences long. I know that kind of goes against what we learned in grammar school about paragraphs and run-on sentences but we need to make sure that people are busy. Our screens are different size settings so if you have something more than four or five sentences long, it looks like a lot of text.

If you break that up just a little bit to keep it between three to four sentences in a long sales letter, or little bits of information, it makes it easier on the eyes. People will stop and read it more because if they're in a hurry, you've got only got two to three seconds to get them to buy something or to get them to interact with your website. If it looks like there's lots of text there, it's like I'm not going to mess with that. I'm just going to go somewhere else where it might be easier. I just want to find out what this is and order it type of scenario.

You want to implement what's called the chunking. Chunk it into smaller groups. We have the wider screens on our websites now, on our laptops and our computers. You want to make sure the text doesn't go all the way from side to side. You want to keep it in a reasonable format so it doesn't look like they're reading back and forth. You definitely don't want to have the page scroll left and right for them to read it. You want to try to make sure it appears that there's not a whole lot of text, even though you can still get your point across if it's chunked correctly.

Something else that doesn't work is not giving them a reason they need your service. Make sure you answer the question as I mentioned earlier, why am I on this site? What will it do for me? Sometimes we say... 'in this ninety minute training, I'll show you how to if you buy my product....' First of all, you have the word 'training' in there that sounds like work. People don't want to work, they want to do it you know. You want to try to make it a little bit more glamorous to them. You want to say things like... 'give me five minutes and I will show you how in this class you can easily increase your income by applying these strategies...' use that type of verbiage instead of training or learning or education type thing. Show them what they're going to get out of it.

You also need to tell people the unique transformation you are offering, you need to do that on your pages. You're spot on with what this is. What are you going to give them for their investment and their time? What are they going to receive just by reading the page? You first want to sell them on your page before you can sell them on the product. You have to get them on that headline and that sub-headline and that first paragraph. You kind of have to sell them as you're going down the page to get them to read a little bit more, read a little bit more, read a little bit more. Those are things you want to do.

One of the biggest things that I see is making sure that they can find what to order. What doesn't work is fancy hyperlinks and order buttons. Many times people use a lot of underlining on their sales letters and you find out that the hyperlinks are the same colour as the underlining and people don't know that they are hyperlinks.

We've been trained all of our web life that hyperlinks are generally blue, or they're a different color and they stand out from the text so we know that we're to click on them. People get away from putting click here to find out more about this product or click here to read more type of scenarios. They just try to be tricky and put a text in here and you're expected to know that it clicks. Those are just a few of the things that I have found that doesn't work. It's not giving them enough information as well.

Attracting People To Your Site

As I mentioned earlier, it is good to give them a free report, a free chapter of your book, an audio clip, a video clip of your training. Have them opt-in and follow up an email series. Most of all explain what they're going to get. Follow up with them.

We've talked about the opt-in box. One of the things that I found actually that helps convert more people is when you have that opt-in box, you want to tell them this is a free report. Tell them what they're going to get. Tell them how to get it and of course, give it to them. All the little details of an opt-in box. See how it just looks like an opt-in box with a name and email address but you want to go into the specifics. Make sure that you say free report given and what the free report is.

I think I had one on my blog originally and I'm going through some transformations on my blog trying to find the right theme that I like. But I had an opt-in that says seven tips to creating your first blog site. Free seven tips to getting your first blog site. I found by adding one of those little certificate circles with the little diagonal borders around it that had free report. I added that and it increased conversions. Also adding the text you say... 'your free report, this is a free report that says you're going to show you how to set up your first blog site.' Below that, you put enter your name and email address and then click the button that reads... 'Get my free seven tips.' Then on the button, there's the name and the email and make sure you have it in the order.

I know this sounds silly and I laughed at it myself at first. But if you say put your name and email below, you don't want the first box to be the email and then the next box be the name. You want it to be specific and this all increases conversion. If you say put in your name and email address below, make sure the first box is the name and the second box is the email. Then click the button that says claim my free report or claim my free seven tips or claim my video sample. Make sure the button says exactly what you say it's going to read. You'd be surprised how much increase you'll see in the conversions just by following those steps. I know it sounds weird and it sounds like well they should know that. Well maybe they don't. Maybe it's their first time online and they're trying to find your product. They don't know what an opt-in box is. They don't know why they're putting in their name and email address. They're afraid of spam. They've heard of people trying to rip off their name and email address so they can be hacked or whatever. You tell them. You're leading them and giving them comfort that they're doing the right thing.

Don't Lose Customers

One of my biggest pet peeves and I'll try not to rant on this one but is to not give them something to click on. Many times when I first started, I wanted to buy something. You get to the bottom of the page, you read all the way through it. You've passed the order box. They've got the little box there that says order now for twenty one days, and there's more text below that. You have the PS and the PPS and then there's more information, and I get below that and there's nothing to click on. There's nothing that takes me back to the order box. There's nothing to say yes I want to go ahead and get this. You have to scroll back up and scrolling, you might pass the order box again or you may not even find it. You just get frustrated and leave. Or you may have links to go to other pages on your website. Maybe you have description of the product that takes them to another portion or you have a multipage website. They click on that and to find out more, maybe you take them to your bio page. They go to your bio page and it tells all about you and yes, they love you and things like that, but there's nothing to click back to go to a product or to find more information or to go to your blog or anything like that. Again, they're lost. You've put them in a dead end and they go somewhere else to buy the product. Make sure that you give them something to click on. That's one of my biggest pet peeves.

I've added videos to some of my longer sales pages. But even after the video, I put the order button below and then I have a sales page under the video because people learn different ways and they like to read different ways. I found that some people watch the video. Other people will skip the video and start reading the sales text or the letter or the copy I have there. You want to build up to the possibility of them buying and people will buy in different stages. You want to give links for them to buy.

Let me try to clarify what I'm meaning here. They're going so far down the page and they're saying yes this is what I want. Do you make them finish reading all the rest of that or do you give them an order link? What I like to do is instead of just giving a link that takes them to the order page, is I like to give them a link that jumps down to the order area. Many times you may give them a bonus. You may give them their satisfaction guaranteed, your thirty day promise or whatever.

What I found is if they click that link and it just takes them to an order page, they may not buy because it's like well what's the return policy? What if I don't like it? If you have them linked, if that link jumps down to an order box where it tells them or reassures them again. It reassures them that yes, I do have a thirty day policy. If you don't like it, I'll buy it back guaranteed type of scenario. You have thirty days to try it. This is everything that you're getting. It gives them a recap of what they're buying and the order button followed by if you're taking credit card, PayPal, or whatever underneath the order button. You're giving them all the information they need in one spot. So, in the sales letter I will provide a few paragraphs and then a link maybe a hyperlink that says yes, this is what I want and I'm ready to order now. But I'll continue with my copy in case they need to buy more. They read a little bit further and instead of a hyperlink, I'll put an order button. I'll transfer back and forth so they see... oh yes, a button is what I want to click on. Maybe they don't know about a hyperlink. On the button it says 'Yes Frank, I'm ready to order now'. They click that and it takes them down to the order box. Integrating that back and forth and always giving them something to click on no matter where they're at increases sales and gives you a better chance of not losing a customer. As I said, giving them instructions like putting on the link or on the button click here I'm ready to order type of scenario. Everybody is in different levels of where they're at online. What you and I have known for years, somebody else may be just starting out and may know what a hyperlink and other such things are.

On Branding

When I first started online and the main reason I went with "That One Web Guy" is just because my last name Deardurff is too hard to say. It's too hard to pronounce on a tele-seminar. We didn't do webinars when I first got online. We were doing tele-seminars and people couldn't hear my last name because of the double F at the end. It sounds like an S. It's just hard to hear. It's hard to spell. It gets typo-ed a lot as you can probably imagine. I kind of went with that 'one web guy' and it became my brand. When they see me at live events, a lot of people say... 'hey it's that one web guy!' The reason I did that because I thought it was kind of catchy. People would say who did your website? Well, that one web guy! It's like "who's on first" type of scenario. It became memorable.

A lot of people, more people than I ever imagined realized that my favourite colour was orange. I did it because I liked it. I started using it in my brand. One of the first things that you think about when you think about Coca-Cola is the colour red. You think of Pepsi, it's blue. When you think of Pizza Hut you think of the red roof. It's the things that they remember whether they think about it or not. If you think about your sales process online, whether using a third party or if you have a cart on your own server or whatever, you want to make sure you're consistent with your branding. Again, it goes back to that comfort level.

If you had your logo and your branding and your colour scheme and they go to an order page and it looks totally different than where they were just at to buy, it's confusing. If they click the order button and it goes to maybe a one shopping cart page that you just left the default white, they're like... 'whoa wait a minute! What just happened here? I'm kind of out of my comfort zone. You want me to put my credit card in where?' If you even just put your logo, (some of the sites make it a little bit more difficult. They're getting better about it) surely you cannot make it look exactly like your website, but by putting your logo or adding your colour or have the colour scheme even kind of match a little bit, your chances of conversion increase. You give them that comfort. It's like yeah, I'm in the right place. I've seen that logo. I was just there. Same way with the auto-responder and the different services you use and with your emails.

Branding is not always about colour and the logos and things. But branding is also like in my case 'Frank - That One Web Guy'. Generally if you get an email from me, it says Frank - That One Web Guy in the form name, it says Frank - That One Web Guy in the closing so they know it's me. I'm trying to add my last name back in there so people recognise that. They may say Frank Deardurff III - That One Web Guy so they can see that, but it's still that one web guy.

I see many marketers or many people online who change that form name. One time it may be from Frank. Next time it may be from Frank Deardurff. Next time it might be Frank - That One Web Guy. Maybe the next time it's Frank Deardurff - That One Web Guy. Maybe the next time it's just That One Web Guy. It changes up. The pattern in their inbox it looks different so they don't always catch it.

Maybe they want to follow everything you have to say. Most cases they don't want to see everything you want to say but you want to be able to see when they look in their inbox that it's from you. They see that pattern. If it's not uniform, it's not consistent you lose your branding. Brands enter their mind that it's from you and they want to know what that is. Branding is a very big part of our marketing and building that long term relationship. 'Mondays with Morri' used to be forever out there and was a big thing. He was known by his message on Monday. It's a consistency. It's funny how people pick these up and tell you about them at live events. I think it's great feedback.

The Next Move

Implement. Do something. I've coached so many people that have bought everything out there. They tell me they bought this product and I find out that they bought three auto-responders and two shopping carts. They have boxes they never opened and things like that. Implement. Do something. Pick one thing and go with it.

Another thing would be to as I said, the three T's. Try, track, and test. Try something, do something. Make sure you apply a new marketing strategy each week. Something, maybe it's just a Tweet a week. Maybe set up a Twitter account and I'm sure if they've followed very long they know how to do that. Set up a Facebook account and tell people about your product or your service. It's not always about telling them about it but letting them know who you are. Just about anybody that follows me on Facebook knows I love my grandkids. They've probably seen pictures of them that I've spent or done something with them. That creates a personality. They know how you are and it creates a trust type of thing with them. Try to implement something and try a new marketing strategy and then track it. Try to find a way to maybe use one of the tracking services to track your links in your emails.

I'm trying a new auto-responder series where it actually tracks every link in my email and I can tell which links were clicked, who clicked what link and things like that. I can track all the way down to every message that I sent out. What was the first click, the second link, the third link? That makes a difference.

Of course testing as we talked about. Test the colours on your website but it's important not to test everything at once because then you don't know what made the change, made the difference. Maybe one week you try changing the colour scheme on the background of your site. Maybe you change it a little bit. Maybe you go from a blue to a little bit of a blue grey. Did that make any difference? No, then change it back to the blue. Maybe change the wording in your header. Do the easy things. Maybe change a few words in your headline to see if it makes a difference. Maybe change the colour of your order buttons. Don't make them all buttons but it may be every second one, change it to a hyperlink instead of a button. See if that makes a difference. Try, track, and test, implement. Do something. Just make sure that you do something.

BUSINESS INNOVATION and CREATIVITY

Sign up and you'll learn how you can innovate and be on the Creative Edge of Innovation and Creativity in Business.
http://crackingtheclientattractioncode.com

CHAPTER ELEVEN

Make A Difference In The World And Have Fun Doing It

BY JEFF HERRING

King of Content Marketing
Content Conversion Secrets
Profitable List Building

"You can get everything in life you want if you will just help enough other people get what they want."

— *Zig Ziglar*

Entrepreneur Magazine has said "When it come to marketing strategies, content marketing has just been crowned king, far surpassing search engine marketing, public relations and even print, television and radio advertising as the preferred marketing tool for today's entrepreneur."

Jeff has been building his own businesses with Content Marketing since 1994. With his exclusive Content Marketing strategies, Jeff has fast become a Living Legend of Quality Traffic Generation.

Jeff has long been the "behind the scenes" guy creating Direct Response Content for many top internet marketers and business leaders, with clients such as Dan Kennedy, Alex Mandossian and others.

Here's what Chris Bloor of Australia said about Jeff after he was a guest on his recent telesummit:

"I can honestly say that in the 12 years I have been online, I have NEVER had anyone leave me wanting more and more of their content than Jeff did in the time he was sharing with me.

I love the feeling you get as you listen to someone and it hits you... "This is going to make a huge difference in my life! I won't be the same after this..."

Discovering The Calling

It's a strange story because it's one of the last things I expected to do. I was originally a marriage and family therapist in a private practice down in Florida, and began writing a relationship column for the local newspaper to promote my practice. This was funny as I never finished my PhD in marriage and family therapy because my professors told me I couldn't write and I believed them. So now I'm writing this column. People kept encouraging me to take that online and teach people how to do it, and finally I did it in 2005 and it just took off.

I was focused on a narrower niche at that time, just article marketing. What I have done since then is expand it into content marketing because content encompasses articles but it's so much more. It could be audio, video, or any combination of the three.

The Unique Transformation

When you're thinking about working with somebody, what is the unique transformation you expect? What I end up doing is attracting people, some that know that they have good content in their head and can get a little bit of it out. Some that can get a lot of it out. Some that can't get any out. Simply stated, I help them unleash and cash in on their content. Unleash that good stuff they know they've got in their heads that can help other people and then cash in on it. This works even when you're trying to get into products, services and/or resources. And be able to do it with a lot of confidence because a lot of people get scared with the steps along the way. They'll create the content and then they get afraid of putting it out there. What if somebody criticises it? My answer to them is... guess what, they will. There are lots of people out there, you know like trolls in their grandmother's basement. So they're trying to take shots at everybody. If you get criticised, what it means is you've been found and that's a good thing!

I also tell people to remember this good quote from Ziglar who once said... "pay little attention to those who criticise for some people the only taste of success they'll ever get is the bite they take out of you". So, get your stuff out there and keep an open heart, develop a thick skin for the criticism because it'll happen. But when you do this in the five parts that I teach of content marketing, the five steps of the transformation, I see people grow. Carla, I watched you grow in such confidence in what you were able to do. I watch my students grow with such confidence, and the beautiful thing is they get their life-changing message out there that can make a difference in the world and they have fun doing it. And they profit from it, it's a pretty good deal!

Attracting New Clients

One of the rules I learned from Dan Kennedy is that the worst number in business is 'one'. I learned this even before I ever heard of Dan Kennedy way back when I was in private practice. I lived in Tallahassee, Florida the capital, there were more therapists than there were cab drivers. Everyone is trying to set themselves apart and that's why I started writing the column. I remember being tempted to stop all my other marketing at that time. I made the very wise decision in hindsight not to because I kept doing all the other marketing that I was doing because that column was in the newspaper. It could go away at any time. It was only supposed to last for six months to a year, it went for ten. But when the local newspapers stopped running it and pulled out, it was still running all around the country, my referrals didn't dry up. I still had all that other marketing out there.

I haven't practiced there for almost ten years now, and but every now and then I get an enquiry about how to make an appointment with me to my email address. I believe this is because people remember that column even though it stopped running locally in that town in '04 or my other marketing.

First thing to do is to have lots of ways to attract clients. One of the main ways is through article content on some of the main article directories like Ezine Articles. That brings me a flood of traffic because any time I put a new article there, it builds on all the others and it just goes into an avalanche. I use YouTube, Facebook, LinkedIn, all those different ways to bring in people.

One of the really, really powerful ways I've been using for a couple of years to bring in new clients and I recommend people do it because it's just so powerful and profitable, is doing affiliate or JV tele-seminars or webinars with other people in your industry. In other words, let's say that you were going to host one of my webinars, I'll create the sign-up page and you take my copy that I send you and make the invitation to everyone. Then they come to my website and opt-in.

Those people have been added to my list. So having a colleague host a webinar for you, or a tele-seminar for you, and have people signing up on your sign-up page builds your list really astronomically. Probably quicker than anything else I've tried. Now, that may not be exactly right. It comes in bigger clumps at one time than all the others, that's for sure. The people that come in, the clients that come in are qualified because they've come to an event, a tele-seminar or a webinar, that's about something specific. So you know they're interested in that something specific. It's a great way to bring in new clients.

Getting the Clients to Say Yes

The great option I mentioned above would be joining a tele-seminar, webinar, getting a freebie from the list versus them to saying yes to invest, which is also a good thing.

While getting them to sign up for stuff, one of the things that I tell people to do is look out there and see what most people are doing and do it differently. Because most people just follow the herd, and most people are broke. What I do, a colleague told me the other day because I teased her about using a similar outline to a subject line of a webinar she was holding. She goes... "heck yeah, I'm going to borrow this stuff! One, you give me permission and two, your emails are so great!"

My answer was, think back to when we both started in 2006 and how many thousands of emails you sent out, you might as well have fun with it. I'm always having fun with my email invitations. Sometimes I'll put in a PS that says this PS was left intentionally blank. Other times I'll put in a small joke. I found a book the other day from 1976. It was all bizarre laws in different states, so I'll list one of those. Some people have told me they open it to see what I'm putting at the bottom.

I don't do a lot of tele-seminars anymore, stick to mostly webinars. One of the things that keep people coming back as regulars is that I make them very, very interactive. I ask them questions that I want them to answer. I ask them to participate. I also do what's called 'results now webinars'. In that they do something on that webinar that helps them create something and make a difference in their business. They're going to achieve something right there.

Anything I do, I try to put a little bit of my personality into it, or a lot of it. Let them know that I've got some resources for them and to put in your personality I think you let them know that they're going to have fun and that you're a fun person.

Think about all those tediously boring webinars and tele-seminars that you've been on when it's just someone spending half an hour talking about themselves and how great they are. Maybe they're really good at what they do, but they don't really know how to present and hold somebody's attention. I'm really big on engaging people and keeping their attention because that's more fun and really when people are having more fun, they're going to spend, they're going to invest with you. It's as simple as that.

Back when I did tele-seminars, I would present it was a show, which I really think they all are if you do it right, a show. I would have episodes of 'what's on Jeff's desk?' And I would just name stuff that's on my desk, like there's a bottle cap there, and five quarters stacked up, and tickets from the John Meyer concert the other night, and on and on. If I didn't do that people would ask for it. Then at that time when I was doing a lot of tele-seminars, I had one of those desk calendars. It was a Monty Python desk calendarandIwouldjustreadfromthat,"readingfromtoday'sMonty Python desk calendar is...." It's got nothing to do with the content I'm delivering, but it's got everything to do with preparing the people for the content I'm delivering because it keeps their attention, it keeps them engaged, and says this is going to be fun.

For most of school, until I got into late college and grad school where I was really taking the classes I wanted, some of those were just painfully boring. I made a promise to myself that if I was ever in a teaching position, and this is long before we knew anything before the Internet, but if I was ever in a teaching position I was going to make it fun. I was going to make it fun for me. I was going to make it fun for them because I think it's a sin to bore people while you teach.

Things That Don't Work

Hard sell stuff doesn't work long term. It might work short term like you hear about all of these sales launches and stuff. What you don't hear about is the return rate, right? The stuff that gets returned. What you don't hear about is the people that don't end up being good clients.

Way back in the 70s in Orlando there was a stereo store, their slogan was 'we don't rub cheese on your neck,' and there was a cartoon of a guy with cheese being rubbed on his neck. The slogan meant we don't high pressure you. People are wary of that.

If you look at any of the calls to action I have where I'm asking you to take an action to invest in something, they're all just invitational. I don't say... "get this tomorrow because it might be taken down, if you just buy tonight because it might be taken down tomorrow, and if you don't your family will starve". Okay, that's a bit of an exaggeration but not by much. And so the hard sell stuff doesn't work long term.

The other thing that doesn't work, and this is the thing that makes people say that email marketing is dead, which it's not. The kind of email marketing that is dead that worked in the beginning was pounding people with a new offer every day. Here's the latest greatest thing that will make you a million dollars! Finally people wizened up and started thinking well, if this is the greatest thing that will make me a million dollars, what happened to the one yesterday that was the greatest thing that was a million dollars? That kind of email marketing is dying out.

The other thing that doesn't work and I see so many people do it is in a lot of different ways, somehow being disingenuous, misleading people, or even lying to people. For example, when I do a webinar it'll be available as a replay for a while, maybe two or three days, then it's available as a webinar we broadcast at various times. It's appointment-based marketing. Many of these webinar rebroadcast systems are set up so that you can make it look like it's live. I do the exact opposite when I announce one. I say this is going to be a webinar re-broadcast, although it will feel live and I'll either be in the background answering questions or I'll answer them before my head hits the pillow that night. So I'm just transparent about it, whereas other people are trying to make it look like it's live. I think lying is a lousy way to start a relationship with a prospect.

The 'Different' Approach

I've always chosen to be different in anything I've done. For instance that column in the newspaper that got all this going, back in the day two or three people had it before me and they would write about terribly uninteresting stuff like what is depression or what is bipolar disorder, very clinical kind of stuff. When I got it I thought I'm just going to write about what happens in my office. I'm not going to name names, but talk about problems, how

I approach problems, and how I solve them. That's what I found really makes your voice online is how you approach and how you solve problems. I think what I learned in dealing face to face with people every day, day in and day out for twenty five years is that it's all about relationships. It's all about connections. Because every now and then, I would just randomly pick a client and sort of do a reverse engineering, how that person got to me, okay? So if that person got to me on a referral from this person, who got to me on a referral from this person who has been a long time client and has referred me like twenty five people because they're a connected person in town.

You just track it back and it's all about relationship even though we don't see each other face to face (now that's coming around with Google hangouts and I'm excited about). Most of the time online we don't see each other face to face so I think it's even more about relationships and it's even more important to pay attention to the relationship. All of this is about relationship building.

That's why I ask people questions like... 'what do you struggle with the most? How can I most help you?' That's why I interact on webinars. That's why I do a lot of what I do so that the relationship is built. I think what really makes this whole thing work is the relationship. That whole thing is relationship based otherwise you're just out there squawking to the air.

Getting Started

My whole thing is to get people creating their content. That's just the beginning of the five parts of the transformation. Following that is online visibility, traffic generation, list building, and product creation, but creating that content that you can use all over the place, repurpose in a lot of different ways is the way to get started.

With the templates, most people think that messes up the creativity, but it actually helps creativity. You can crank out so much content and plus you get a bonus on re-purposing. You get a bonus of a strategy session, which is me on the phone, taking a look at your content and seeing how far we can take it, and beginning to build your content empire.

So that's an awesome way to get started. I would say that would be a good entry level for us to start working together and see how big we can take your content, your expertise.

The Final Thoughts

I would just like to encourage everybody... you didn't get on here because you have nothing else to do, you've got a dream of building a practice and making a difference with people and I would encourage you to simply start. You may not feel ready, but you will get more ready as you go. Simply start, take your chances, get your elbows and knees skinned. Learn to keep doing it. Take repeated action.

I have a friend, Paul Evans who put a new meaning on ADD. He calls ADD 'Action is Done Daily'. You just do this stuff consistently over time and it builds and builds and builds. Because two things I really believe folks and take this to heart. One, no one ever fails online. Some people just give up before the magic happens. And the second thing is, folks let this one really sink in... there are more people out there waiting to hear your message who can only hear it from you than you can ever get to in your lifetime.

That means if you're in a crowded niche, there are plenty of people out there for you. So get your stuff out there. Get your message out there. Start making a difference in the lives of the people you were called to serve and making a profit from it, which is a great way to go about living.

YOU'RE ALMOST THERE!

Chuck Yeager was the first person to break the sound barrier. Here's what he said: Ät the moment of truth, there are either reasons or results."

Are you ready for your breakthrough?

http://crackingtheclientattractioncode.com

Your Potential Customers & Clients Are Using Social Media, You Must Be There Too!

BY *CARLA MCNEIL*
Chief Social Butterfly at Butterfly Networking
Social Media Manager

"It takes 20 years to build a reputation and five minutes to ruin it. If you think about that, you'll do things differently."

—Warren Buffett

A number of years ago I was participated in a coaching program with Loral Langemeier. I signed up because I wanted to make my multilevel marketing business grow. I was looking on-line to find people because I had a day job and found getting out to meet people challenging. I discovered I really liked working online, so I learned LOTS more. One of the benefits of Loral's coaching program was we met in person four times a year with the group, about fifty people. When it came to the questions regarding online strategies, tactics and how to's, everybody kept asking me. Carla will you help me do this? Carla will you show me how to do this? Will you do it for me? And I kept saying no. I would work with people while we were there in session but that wasn't my business. I was interested in doing all of that on-line stuff, but not as a business.

This went on for about a year and a half and finally the universe hit up the side of the head hard enough with that 2X4 that I realized wait a minute, I love doing this stuff, why don't you say yes Carla? That was when I finally started saying yes and Butterfly Networking was born.

I was doing all of these things and I was delving deep into internet marketing, I've had a number of different teachers from the high level strategy types right down to the click here, click here, click here types of instructors. And it was amazing when I finally did switch how things started to flow better.

The one thing with the whole social media platform is that it does change constantly. I know last night I was working with a couple of members of my team and they're asking questions about, Facebook and Twitter. I said wait thirty minutes and it will probably start working again. And sure enough it did. Simply because they're making so many changes on their platforms that it can be very difficult to keep up. Which is one of the reasons that I am always taking some sort of a training program. And it's very unusual for me not to be on like a webinar of some sort every second or third day. That's how much training it takes for me to keep up with what's going on social media all the time.

The Unique Transformation

Our main focus lies in managing social media for small business owners. What we provide is a realization that you really can get qualified leads from social media. It does work, it does take time and effort and in a lot of cases dollars, in order to make that happen. Marketing on social media is easy, it's really easy to get out there and make a post and stuff like that. But to do it right is not always easy. There are a number of different things that have a big impact to your audience.

One little tidbit with Facebook, if you go to my page http://facebook.com/butteflynetworking/, you will notice we do not do posts without pictures. The reason, people will stop and look at pictures where they rarely stop and look at just text. They'll be scrolling through their news feed or scrolling down their page, and they'll stop at pictures.

At an event I was sitting at a table between two clients, we were watching the presentation at the front of the room. Both of them I guess got bored with what was happening at the front of the room so they opened the Facebook tab on their computers. And that's exactly what they were doing; they were scroll, scroll, scroll, stop at a picture. If it was an interesting picture they took a look. And then they were, scroll, scroll, stop some more, stop, another interesting picture. It got to the point where both of them were scrolling and stopping in unison. So then I wasn't paying attention to the front of the room either, but it was a real eye opener to me just how impactful those pictures were. So whenever you make a post on Facebook include a picture.

As the geek who is always learning I find ways all the time to make social media more effective and cost less. I'm always Tweeting, I'm always learning. That really is the bigger unique transformation that we deliver. It's about testing for your specific product, for your specific niche. You can start out doing what other people are doing but you are definitely going to have to narrow things in and discover what works for your specific audience. We all attract audience. In less than a year we've got 150,000 likes on our Facebook page. We used to have a service where we would guarantee 10,000 Facebook likes in ninety days, but as I said the platforms are changing constantly and that strategy no longer works. Facebook changed the rules.

Attracting Clients

I personally have found the best way to attract clients is to be out there talking to people, answering questions and posting good information. What works best for me personally in my business is the combination of meeting people at events, whether they are local, long distance or online events. I make sure that I connect with as many people as I can from each different event.

I take all of the business cards and contact information that I receive from people and go to Twitter, Facebook, LinkedIn, YouTube and find them. Then I send each and everyone we can find friend requests or connection request and subscribe to their YouTube channels. I make sure I stay connected. When you're connected on all the different platforms and **your personal profile picture is the same** on all of them, and you are branding. It doesn't have to be official branding but maybe just the colors that you use, that's consistent, and people will then go... "Oh I recognize her, Oh I recognize him". That way people will like and trust you more than they would, had they just met you at the event and you sent them an email.

When you take the time and add that whole connection piece on social media, you're actually putting yourself in front of your target market a lot more often. Depending on who you speak to, it can take anywhere from seven to twelve touches before a potential client will buy.

Social media helps to speed up that process and demonstrate your trustworthiness. But, and it's a BIG but, one of the things that I strongly recommend is that if you don't have the time to go in on all of those different platforms and be consistent with your posting and interaction, then don't start. Because there's nothing worse than starting to rely on someone and then they disappear. All that trust, all of that disappears and you have to start all over again. But if you don't have time to do all of them then concentrate on the one or the two that are going to be the most effective for your business.

Facebook for Coaches and Healers.

People spend more time personally on Facebook than they do on the other platforms. People go onto Facebook to find out what their friends are doing, to catch up on different things that are happening in their neighborhood. Maybe some events, maybe they belong to a bunch of different groups. They go onto Facebook for social reasons, for fun reasons. So when you go there as coach or healer people are more likely to find you in that fun/social mindset. Twitter is more about speed and LinkedIn is more about business, not the best platforms for a coach or healer to start. When I'm working with healers and coaches, yes you may have a lot of potential on LinkedIn and I might suggest depending on what type of a coach you are LinkedIn might be your first choice, but for most it will be your backup. However, because people are going to Facebook for coaches and healers, it is the best place to start. There are over a billion people on Facebook; your market is there. It's just a matter of dialing in and finding them.

Based on the Facebook Terms and Conditions you must have a personal profile in order to create a page. However, you cannot sell from your personal profile. You can make offers to people by inviting them to events or offer something for free that leads them over to your Facebook page. There are many different strategies you can use to move people from your personal profile over to your Facebook page but you cannot put a blatant offer of any sort on your personal profile or Facebook just might shut you down.

You can advertise your classes on your personal profile. When the link to the classes is taking them off Facebook and they're going somewhere else to sign up for the class, that's okay. You can also use the events within Facebook itself. But it depends on whether or not you're charging for your class. If you're charging for your class then it is not a good idea. I suggest a free class to attract clients to you, a great lead generation strategy. I do a free webinar every month on different social media topics; the reason is to attract more clients. You can put something like that on your personal profile but if you're going to be doing some direct selling, no don't do it from your personal profile.

Groups- you can sell from your group, you can insert links to offers in the group feed. I'm in a number of different groups that are always offering us different things. There are two different kinds of groups; private ones and public. It just depends on your market and you've got to do your research and find out whether or not those groups are right for you. The groups I belong to are all private ones and a few open ones on Facebook. Be selective in what you join as they can become VERY time consuming!

Attracting Clients

I have a lot of videos on my YouTube channel and it's a great way to attract potential clients. The YouTube channels' got a weird name it's my old MLM name, it's 'youtube.com/retirewithcarla'. There are over a hundred videos on the channel that show you how to do different things on social media; step by step. Our most popular which has over 15,000 views on 'How To Unfriend A Friend on Facebook'. Some of the other titles are 'How To Create A Facebook Group', 'How To Create A List On Twitter', 'How To Set Up Your Own YouTube Video'. There are lots of free videos on the channel.

The other thing that I find is very effective is article marketing. And I don't write as many articles as I would like these days, priorities. I use http://ezinearticles.com it's where I publish my articles and I am currently #4 top Ezine Article writer for social medial marketing. Ezine Articles gets millions of hits a month and it's the leading Article platform on the Internet. If you have not yet created a lot of content, Ezine Articles is where you can go and find content. You can use the content that's on Ezine Articles, provided you give credit where credit is due to the person who has written it. But you could do a blog post on someone else's article. You would simply add your own comments about the article. I use Twitter every day to send people to relevant articles I wrote a long time ago and they bring me traffic all the time.

Content is King

Content is what Google thrives on. If you want to be found organically you've got to be feeding the Google machine and you feed the Google machine with content. The added benefit of all of that content is people can figure out who I am before they make a decision. I publish articles on a regular basis, I post on my blog regularly, and I post on my social media platforms regularly; people can so tell I'm consistent, which also means I'm reliable. From the actual content itself you can tell that I know what I'm talking about. So it's two fold. They can get to know you, they can get to like and trust you, and it also benefits your search engine optimization; making sure you can be found organically. The more you create content, you're having your calling card those many places on the internet, which results in people finding you when they do a search.

Q & A

Q: I'm an attorney who represents new and emerging business as they're outside general counsel and business development for a flat monthly charge, which increases over time as my clients' business grows. How can I meet these types of companies through social media to let them know I am here to support them in this way?

The best platform for someone in that area would be LinkedIn. You're going to find the small business owners in the various different groups on LinkedIn. So build out your LinkedIn profile, make sure that you fill in absolutely everything because everything is searchable. Also find groups that are connected in some way to your target market. Find groups of small business owners in your local area if you are only providing service in a small area and answer questions or pose questions to people. Lots of times people don't know what they need to ask. If I were looking for a lawyer here in the Vancouver area, I'd be only looking at someone who demonstrated they were knowledgeable in the area of on-line marketing. (there's not many out there). Decide what niche you want to be in and specifically look for those groups. If you, as the lawyer can go into some of these different groups and pose the questions or make comments that answer their questions you'll be setting yourself up as the expert, the "go to" lawyer. Get in there and have those conversations. That will really really help.

Q: *I'm just about to put myself out there so there's a lot of discomfort and one of my fears is that I tend to drag on and talk too much. And so how do I polish up my presentation, not only electronically like on Facebook and LinkedIn but also when people want to talk to me, or if I want to answer questions. Do you have some guidelines to keep it short and sweet and yet effective because I tend to just drag on and on like I'm doing right now?*

I'm the exact opposite. I can sometimes be too short and not go into enough detail, which in some ways is also good. Remember when you write from the perspective of the reader and when we're on-line we want things in short snippets. It's like "just tell me what I need and I'm moving on". Even videos don't work when they really long. Videos need to be short, less than two minutes. If you can answer the question in one paragraph, as little as two sentences or as many as five that would be awesome. Always stop and think of it in the time chunk of your reader. When they're going on-line to read something it's normally for a short period. Remember reading doesn't hold their attention as well as a video does. So you need to be really concise. If you're in a business where you're offering a free strategy, or you have something that answers the question even better over on your website, tell people... "You know what this is a really great question, people ask me that question often, in fact so much so that I have made an entire blog post on it, go here (insert your link) and take a look".

You don't necessarily have to blog. You could be sending them over to your Facebook page to find the answer. That is one of the things that you also want to do and one of the reasons I am such a firm believer in article marketing; I can take those questions, write an article on it and I can post it everywhere. I use the articles on my Facebook page, Twitter, and LinkedIn. I can send people to a specific article to answer a specific question so that I'm not constantly answering the same question over and over again.

If you are a bit frustrated because they keep asking the same questions or very similar questions, then you definitely need to have a place where you can answer those questions and when they come back to you just send them to it.

If some people you work with don't use the internet, Facebook or anything like that, then they need to pay you to have a session with you. If they're taking your time and drawing upon all of the knowledge that you have invested lots of time, money and energy to obtain, develop and nurture they need to be paying for your time.

Q: So is there any other techniques or anything that you could give me to keep it concise and short even in polishing up my presentation as well when I have, when I interview or when I'm trying to put little spurts of information out there in the media?

My suggestion would be to write it like you normally would and edit it down by half. Be brutal with yourself.

Don't Hard Sell

I don't like pitch fests. I like building relationships and providing value. It makes for a much longer lasting relationship. I am a social media manager. We want to have clients for years, we don't want to have a client for one month and do all that up front work and have them disappear. It's not a good business model. Coaching is the same, you don't want people to come in the door and coach with you for one hour and never come back again because we know that's never enough. As human beings we all have foibles and blocks and different things that we allow to take ourselves out. We know that takes more than an hour.

If you're going in for a pitch fest and all you're doing is going after the dollar, after the dollar, after the dollar without building the relationship it's going to be a lot more work. In the long run, building the relationships, providing that value is a much easier way to go.

Pictures Speak a Thousand Words

If you're business model is product based direct marketing a combination of Facebook and Pinterest would be the two social media platforms to concentrate on. In fact I have an Avon client and for her I strongly recommended Facebook and Pinterest, the basic reason being... pictures. Pictures create more of a draw to those products and people stop at pictures they often don't stop and look at text. That's why Pinterest has done so well.

When you take a look at the Alexa Ranking, (Alexa Ranking is where they rank all of the different websites that exist on the web) Google is #1 Facebook is #2 and all of the other mainstream social media platforms are in the top twenty. That tells you that you need to be taking advantage and leveraging of all the traffic those sites get. If your business uses lots of pictures like an Avon business, I would definitely recommend taking a close look at Pinterest and Facebook. Even if you believe your business does not have a lot of picture potential take some time to think about how you can use pictures. Maybe your product in action, demonstrate the benefits of your product or perhaps the results of your product. I know someone who sells spatulas and they make videos that feature their product in use. They are quite popular!

Inspiring Clients to Say 'YES'

Ask lots of questions. I used to be a person who would go out and get so excited that if you would ask me one question, I'd vomit the answer all over you. I would tell you how to do things and go on and on and on. But I learned that that doesn't work, it mostly scares people away. What they need is an understanding that you are going to be able to help them be more. Whatever your business is, for me it is more leads, for coaches it's more changes in your life, more, whatever you're coaching for. But the whole concept is that we are going to be able to provide them more, abundance. And asking questions makes a huge difference, a very huge difference. It has changed my closing rate. I went from someone who used to blurt out anything and everything to someone who asks more questions.

A free report on "7 Facebook Rules That Could Ruin Your Business" http://crackingtheclientattractioncode.com

---

CHAPTER THIRTEEN

Three Steps To Create Money

BY NILOFER SAFDAR
Money and Prosperity Coach
Host Illusion to Illumination Summit
Access Consciousness Certified Facilitator CFMW

"Sometimes questions are more important than answers."

—*Nancy Willard*

I always knew that there was this piece about making money which had nothing to do with what you were doing. So I would look at people all my life doing things, and then I would see some other people doing the same things and some of them would be more successful than the others. I always used to wonder to myself what is it that allows one person doing the same thing to make much more money than the other. That started off my enquiry into this whole realm.

I started to read all kinds of books. I read books on Law of Attraction, I read books on creating money, creating prosperity, and every book that I read it just felt... yes that is true, it should be possible like that. But no matter what tools I used it didn't work as well as it should have worked. For a long time I kept exploring this topic and I just knew there was so much more possible there, but I didn't know how to get there until I found Access Consciousness about two years ago and I started to apply the tools of access consciousness.

I attended an Access Consciousness Workshop and at the end of the workshop I said, "You know what, everything in my business has to change, everything in my money situation has to change and I am now going to create more money than I ever created before".

I started to take the tools of Access Consciousness and apply them to my business to create and generate more money for my business. In one year or rather half a year I created more money in business than I have ever had in my whole life before.

Three Steps to Wealth Creation

I know that these steps are going to sound a little too easy for people so my invitation is use them. Literally, give yourself ninety days, use the steps that I share with you and see what changes for you. I mean the worst thing that can happen is that you would have spent about fifteen, twenty minutes every day doing a bunch of things and you know nothing might change, but the best thing that can happen is that everything can change and you will know that money never has to be an issue in your life any more.

Step One - Have your Target

Now this can seem to be very easy to people, so first of all don't call it goal, because one of the dictionary meanings of goal, G, O, A, L, is jail. You don't want to create the energy of a jail for yourself. Instead you can call them targets. You can keep aiming for your targets over and over again and it will not stick you if you have not yet achieved it. Now here's the thing about targets. Having come from an eastern background I had this whole point of view that you have to be happy with what you have. So I would look at the kind of money that I had available to me and I would go, "Oh I have all this money and that's enough for me. My husband provides for me and I don't really require too much more money so this is enough". I had bought into that story of I should be happy with what I have. As a result that created for me kind of a situation where money never grew. Until one fine day I realised that there's nothing wrong in wanting to have more, and when I actually create more for my-self then I can create a whole lot of change in other people's lives because I am willing to have more money. So I changed my point of view around that and I started to have bigger targets.

One of the things with targets is that you have to keep creating new targets all the time. I have a strategy - every New Year's Eve I sit down and I write out my targets for the whole year. Then I look at those targets every three months, and I will create new ones if I'm already achieving the targets that I have set out, or if some of those targets are no longer in line with where I'm going then I'll change them. Have a plan and sit and create new targets periodically. You can do it once per year or you can do it every quarterly, or you can do it every month. My target with this is to be able to do it every month. I haven't yet got around to doing that, but that's next on my target.

The other thing about targets is you can have targets which seem to be achievable to you. You can also have targets which will actually put you out of your comfort zone so it's a little out there, a stretch for you to achieve them. Then have those targets which are way beyond. You know that target, that when you look at it is so huge that you cannot in your mind compute how you're going to achieve it. But have those targets.

Why is it important to have targets in these three ways? When you set targets which are achievable to you and you start achieving those targets what happens is you tend to have this reconnection going on in your brain... 'I'm setting my targets and I'm achieving my targets, I'm setting my targets and I'm achieving my targets'. Then there are those targets which are going to be a little bit more of a stretch for you. Now these are the targets which are most tricky, because it's like you know it's possible but at the same time it's like a stretch for you. But what happens with these is that you're always trying to make it into an achievable target. So you're trying to create those systems and processes in order to achieve them. And then there is the third target which is like way out there. You look at it and you look at where you're right now and you cannot fix it in any way. The only thing that you can do with those targets is to just let them be. And that's where the magic actually starts to occur, because when you have those targets which are so big, which are so huge that you don't know how you're going to achieve them, then you have to go into this place of 'absolute creation' which is nothing to do with doing. You have to let go of your whole story of I have to do this, this and this in order to achieve this because you know that nothing that you do is actually going to help you get there. But it kind of puts that target in that place of... 'Wow I wonder what it would be like to be able to create that'?

So you have that big target in front of you, but when you look at it or when you write it down you think, 'Well other people can have that but not me, I don't know how to do that'. No matter what you look at in your universe as in terms of what you have done in the past, none of that is going to help you achieve that because its way out there for you.

What that creates for you in your universe is, "Oh I don't have something which is going to help me create that". So you have to shift from that place of what I know to what I don't know. If you don't know something do you then become willing to know it, or to create it instead of creating from I know?

If you look at the energy of I know, it's like I know can only help you create what you know. But if you are trying to create something that you don't know, then you actually have to use the energy of I don't know to create it.

What actually happens is that you start to become a little more comfortable in this energy of 'I don't know'. All creation will happen in that energy from I don't know because that is the energy where all the possibilities exist, where you have all these infinite possibilities and you can choose things, you can create things from that place.

Now the other thing with targets that you can be aware of is that you will often go into this place of oh my God I have to create this which is what I call the vested interest. It's fine to have the vested interest in things but just be aware of it. You can go wow, I would like to create this target and I have a really big vested interest in this. You just become aware of your vested interest and the extent to which you can let go of that vested interest and operate from a place of needless-ness, and be okay with never reaching that target, the more likely that you are going to achieve that target.

If you can't let go, its fine for now but you'll be aware that that's where you're at. I have a vested interest in achieving this, Oh I'm operating from a place of neediness in achieving this. Just have that awareness. Have the small targets and have the way big targets where you just cannot seem to just fix things.

Step Two – Being in the Question

This is the most fun step. Being in the question means that you have to ask a question, but you are not going to look for an answer. When you first start working with this, it's going to be a little difficult because all our lives we've been programmed to believe that you have to find the right answer for things. So the moment I ask a question my first thing is to go into finding the right answer for it. But just for the sake of our exercise, let go of the need to find the answer and just be in the question. The number one thing which is going to help you in creating your target is being in the question.

What kind of questions do you ask? You can ask who, what, where, when, how question, but you cannot ask why questions. The reason why you cannot ask why questions is, notice when you ask the why question it will keep you going around in circles. It's like a snake eating its own tail. So you can ask any other question except a why question.

I'm going to share with you two questions which can help you to actually create things The first question is, 'What would it take for me to have this? Or what would it take for this to show up'? And the second question is 'What can I be or do different today to create this right away'?

Let's say one of your targets is to go to an event with Lisa Sassevich in Los Angeles in a couple of weeks. Write this down in the framework of the questions I've given you. So you could write 'What would it take for me to go to X, Y, Z event with Lisa Sassevich in LA in two weeks? The other way you could write it out is 'What can I be or do different today to go to Lisa Sassevich's event right away'?

Now when you read the question it doesn't feel so overwhelming. It pulls you out from that place of, 'Oh my God I need to do this and this is not happening and I don't know how this is going to happen', and all those conversations that you're having. It puts you in this place of almost I call it settledness which says what would it take for me to go there I wonder. It's like an expansive energy which creates a forward movement for you. Now when you look at it and even if you still have the vested interest in it, just the fact that you wrote it down as a question will help you to create much more than just having it written down as a target.

One of my favourite questions to ask is 'How does it get any better than this'? This is a question you ask if something bad happens and you can use it because you want to create something better than that. If something good happens you can still use it because you want to create something better than good.

No matter what you're creating, no matter what is showing up in your life, start using the question 'How does it get any better than this'?

The other question that I wanted to share with you is 'What else is possible here'? Now this is my favourite question of all time because we live in this no choice universe and we don't want to give ourselves more than two choices, maximum three choices. So we look at all these situations going on in our life and business which are very sticky and we kind of jump to conclusions 'Oh my God this is never going to change and I'm going to have this for the rest of my life'. Or you go to this place of,"Oh no not again, this thing is happening again. So in those places you say 'What else is possible here that I haven't even considered'?

The best thing to do especially if something is really tough and you are stuck in this place and you're unable to change it, use the questions like a mantra. So everything in that situation comes to your awareness. Say the question fifteen, twenty times, say if fifty times, say it a hundred times and by the time you have repeated it over and over again, what you are going to notice is that the energy changes and you start to be much more in this place of peace and allowing and receiving . So use the question.

Literally I can have sticky situation going on in my life and I can just go what else is possible here, what else is possible here, what else is possible here, what else is possible here? And by the time I've done it fifteen, twenty times, that sticky energy is gone and I start to see new choices in that situation, I start to see new possibilities there.

Another question you can use is 'What am I choosing now that is creating this and what else can I choose', because everything that you're creating in your life is result of a choice you're making. So when a choice you're making is not working out for you all you have to do is choose something new. If you ask this question, something starts to shift for you energetically and you start to see new choices available to you.

The other question you can ask is 'What question can I ask here to shift this'? It's as simple as that. Again I noticed when I first started using this tool I was all about 'Oh my God I need to find the right question to ask so that I can create this or this situation can change'. But what if it was not about a right question, what if it was just about being in question no matter what your question is? So literally you don't have to create a super fantastic question or something, you can use the simplest of questions and you can start to shift and change things for you.

The new question that I'm playing with these days is 'What are the infinite possibilities in

this'? Another variation of 'How does it get any better than this is "How can this turn out to be even greater than I could have expected"? Ask the question, don't look for an answer.

Now one of the things that you have to look for about being in question is often we have a statement with a question mark attached. You don't want to do that because that is a place where again you start to create from 'I know' instead of the energy of 'I don't know'. So just be aware of the question you are asking.

Let me give you an example about statements with a question mark attached. You know as a mother I would ask my kids, "So what do you want to have for dinner"? Notice in this there's already an assumption that my kids want to have dinner. I'm asking them "What do you want to have for dinner", instead of actually asking them "Are you hungry? Would you like to eat now"? You don't want to do that. Whatever it is, even if you begin by using a statement with a question mark attached it's going to create way more in your

Universe than you creating from a place of answers. So be in the question. Use the questions that I have given you.

Now let me give you a question for creating more money. Who would like that?

What can I be or do different today to create money for me and my business right away?

Another really fun question and I love being in this question. 'What would it take for me to have never enough money and more money than I can ever spend'? It's literally taking you to that place of never having enough money and always having more money than you can ever spend. And since I started being in that question that's actually what's starting to show up in my life.

So literally this is what I did the whole of last year. For three months and more than that, I wrote down all my targets, I converted each one of my targets into a question and I started reading those questions every single day. Sometimes you can be in that question, you can repeat that question a multiple number of times. So that's step number two, being in the question.

Step Three - Gratitude

You must have heard this so many times from all kinds of teachers, coaches and mentors about the importance of gratitude. I would hear people say that and I would say I will do it one fine day and I never actually got round to doing that until one of my friends started this thing called The Twenty One Day Gratitude Challenge. The Gratitude Challenge was that for twenty one days you had to write down ten new things that you are grateful for today. I started writing my gratitude journal too. I have an iPhone and the first thing that I would do when I woke up in the mornings was to write down in my gratitude list ten new things I'm grateful for today. When you start writing ten new things you're grateful for each day, what happens is you start to look at all the things which happen to you which you are grateful for and you start to shift from this place of 'Oh my God I don't have, I don't have, I don't have', to this place of 'Oh wow! I have so much'. You start to see all the miracles which are showing up for you, the magic that is showing up for you and you start to acknowledge it, you start to be grateful for it.

I would be writing and I would be reading my questions every single day. I would keep adding to my questions because I would go to this place of 'I would like to create this' almost every single day and when I read it after few days or I read it after a couple of weeks, I would look at one of the questions and I would go,"Oh my God this is happening!!!', or 'oh my God this is on the way to happening or I have already received it'. So it's like 'Wow how cool is that I created that in my life'. That is something I can add to my gratitude list. You start to notice all the magic which is showing up for you and you're starting to be in this energy 'I have so much and I'm so happy'.

When you have to write down ten new things that you're grateful for, not only will you just write it down but you will have that gratitude show up in your whole being. What that did to me is it totally shifted me into this place for 'wow I have so much'. If you're functioning from 'I have so much', you start to be an invitation to have more show up in your life. Whereas if you're functioning from this place of 'oh my God I don't have enough I don't have enough, I don't have enough' guess what you're creating? You're just creating 'I don't have enough'.

I did these three things for ninety days and after ninety days everything started to change in my business in terms of money and since then I have now created more in my business than I have ever done before in my life.

Step One Target

Step Two Questions

Step Three Gratitude.

TQG

You will create change if you start to use the tools. You won't believe the number of people I share this information with and I believe there will be a few in those people who will take this information and will start to apply this information in their lives.

I actually shared these questions with one of my clients a few months ago and a month back I got a call from her and she told me that everything had changed in her life. Not only did she take this and apply it to her business, but she had a lot of stuff going on in her body. She called me and said "I used these questions like a hundred times every day and things in my body that I never ever thought would ever change like psoriasis and excess weight all changed". She had lost four kilos in twenty days and she said that the chemical composition of her skin changed and that the psoriasis too was changing. She finally found out that the medication that she had been using for her thyroid disorder was creating all these things as a side effect in her body. And she's been taking that medication for sixteen years now, that's what happens when you start going into question.

What happens is you start to be aware of new information. Once you have the new information you can change this. So literally by being in the question she now has access to that new information which is going to help her create even more change in her body.

So this is just an example of how using these tools she's been able to create change in her body. I can give you so many examples of people who have used these tools and created change in their business, in their money flows, how much I have changed in my own situation.

There was this event that I wanted to go to and it was a lot of money at that point for me. And I looked at it and I went 'I would love to go for this event but I just don't have the money for it'. All I did was that I went into question with that and I created a whole set of questions around that and I would read those questions every single day. In the end I created the money to go to the event.

So it's like whatever you would like to create, use the tools. If you don't use it, you're going to read this and go 'Oh that's good information that's interesting', you'll be motivated for a bit. I call motivation as water off a ducks back. As long as the duck is in the water, it's in the water, the moment it's out of the water it's all gone. So if you're trying to create change in your life, use the tools I've shared with you.

You become that whole energy of 'I have so much and thank you'. It puts you in that place of needlessness. Remember we were talking about having a vested interest, the more you start to use the tools, you'll notice that the vested interest, the neediness just starts to fall away because you start to be aware of just how much is already in your life and you start acknowledging all those things that you do have going on in your life.

One of the questions that I have been functioning from for over a year now is," What would I like to create my life as"? Functioning from this one question I have been able to create more in my life, create more in my business, create more in my body, create more in my relationships than I ever have before in my life.

GET FREE CALLS FROM "HOW TO BECOME MONEY WORKBOOK SERIES"

http://crackingtheclientattractioncode.com

Who is Carla McNeil?

Carla, a social media expert, guides you through the maze of Facebook, Twitter, LinkedIn and YouTube. Based on Carla's expertise with social media, she can help you...

- Find your customers & clients

- Build relationships

- Sell your products & services

- And more...

Carla McNeil, the leading international social media manager helps you make money with your social media campaigns on Facebook LinkedIn, Twitter, and YouTube.

Born and raised in a tiny fishing village on Northern Vancouver Island, British Columbia, Canada, a community called Alert Bay.

Before social media came along, Carla worked in everything from selling Avon products to teaching sewing to consulting in the hospitality industry. May sound like she's tried a bit of everything but every job, profession and career Carla's engaged in has been about networking and being social. That's what social media marketing is all about and it fits Carla to a T!

Trained by the best in internet marketing, Carla fast became a geek who loves to teach, especially when it comes to social media marketing. Along the way, Carla realized the power and fun of Facebook, Twitter, and YouTube. Discovered that chatting, networking and socializing on the internet is profitable... if you know what you're doing. Carla knows what she's doing.

She's helped her clients find customers and clients, build relationships, and sell more products and services with social media marketing. She can manage your social media marketing campaign or she can teach you how to do it yourself. It's up to you.

Carla, a prolific writer, has written dozens of online articles showing business people and entrepreneurs how to use social media marketing to gain customers and clients.

Owner of a membership site that teaches you the ins and outs of social media (SM) and search engine optimization (SEO). A place where you can discover the latest tips and techniques to keep you ahead of the game of SM and SEO.

To contact Carla for further information about her training programs and consultancy or to schedule her for a presentation, please write to:

carla@butterflynetworking.com
Toll Free: 1-877-767-7544
Website: www.ButterflyNetworking.com

Who is Nilofer Safdar?

Nilofer Safdar is a bestselling author of the book, Cracking the Client Attraction Code. Her book was a #1 Bestseller in 3 categories on Amazon and a Hot New Release in 4 Categories. She teaches people how to write, be published and become a Bestselling Author in 90 days even if they have never written before (or think that they can never write). She is a strong advocate of getting a book published and her pet peeve is to educate people on why everyone must write a book.

She is the host of a TV show which aired on JIA News in India called The Nilofer Show.

She is the host of the First online radio show in the Middle East, The Healthy Living Dubai Show, in which she interviews Speakers, Coaches, Natural Healers from the Middle East which empowers the listeners to Create everything they desire in life.

She is also the host of the telesummit, Illusion to Illumination Summit, in which she has interviewed more than 150 Luminaries, Change Agents, Best Selling Authors from around the world including Peggy Phoenix Dubro, the originator of the EMF Balancing Technique, Gary Douglas – the founder of Access Consciousness.

Nilofer helps people change their reality to generate and create a life they desire and require. Her target is to generate a life that is joyful and expansive for everybody she touches.

Nilofer is a Life Coach, Money Mastery Coach, Public Speaking Coach, Relationship Coach and Weight Loss and Anti Aging Expert.

To contact Nilofer for further information about her books, audios, newsletters, workshops & training programs and consultancy or to schedule her for a presentation, please write to:

nilofer@illusiontoilluminationsummit.com
Websites are –

www.illusiontoilluminationsummit.com

www.healthylivingdubai.com

www.nilofersafdar.com

About the Contributors

Gary Douglas
Website: www.AccessConsciousness.com & www.GaryMDouglas.com
Email: Gary@AccessConsciousness.com

Craig Duswalt
Website: www.CraigDuswalt.com
Email: craig@craigduswalt.com
Telephone: 818-735-9900

Amethyst Wyldfyre
Website: www.theempoweredmessenger.com
Email: amethyst@theempoweredmessenger.com
Telephone: 603-594-2744

P J Van Hulle
Website: www.RealrPosperityInc.com
Email: info@realprosperityinc.com
Telephone: 925-289-8047

Dana Garrison
Website: www.danagarrison.com
Email: info@danagarrison.com

Tracey Fieber
Website: www.TraceyFieber.com
Email: contact@traceyfieber.com
Telephone: 306-636-2484

Heather Picken
Website: www.HeatherPicken.com
Telephone: 888-775-2224

Samantha Bennett
Website: www.TheOrganizedArtistCompany.com & www.TheOrganizedEntrepreneurCompany.com

Erika Kalmar
Website: www.GiveawayForCoaches.com & http://www.getreadytocoach.com/

Frank Deardurff
Website: www.FrankDeardurff.com

Jeff Herring
Website: www.JeffHerring.com
Email: support@JeffHerring.com

Carla McNeil
Website: www.ButterflyNetworking.com
Carla@ButterflyNetworking.com
Toll Free:1-877-767-7544

Nilofer Safdar
Website: www.illusiontoilluminationsummit.com & www.nilofersafdar.com
Email: nilofer@illusiontoilluminationsummit.com

Gifts from Contributors

Gary Douglas
Free download of Chapter 1 of best-selling book, "The Place" written by Gary Douglas
http://garymdouglas.com/

Craig Duswalt
Craig Duswalt has a very special offer for you over on http://www.rockstarmarketingbootcamp.com

Amethyst Wyldfyre
Free Gift - "When Money's Tight" Audio Training plus Ezine Subscription:
http://www.theempoweredmessenger.com/gifts

P J Van Hulle
"FREE Access to 21 Hot Video Tips"
"Learn How to Overcome the Greatest Challenges Most Coaches, Consultants, and Speakers Face When It Comes to Attracting More Clients."
http://www.realprosperityinc.com/

Dana Garrison

To see which Entanglements and Imprints are affecting you, to have conscious mind and unconscious mind breakthroughs, and to experience some Family Disentanglement and Childhood Re-Imprinting sessions, get the online course on Entanglements and Imprints for free:
www.danagarrison.com/you-got-gifted

Tracey Fieber
For questions or package information, please book a complimentary discussion and discover the edge Tracey Fieber Business Solutions offers your company. Send an email to contact@tracey-fieber.com

Heather Picken

"What are the problems and what can I do to help solve them?" Want the rest of the Secrets? Download your copy here: https://heatherpicken.leadpages.net/empressonlinefreebook/

Erika Kalmar

Check out – "How to add 3,000+ targeted prospects to your list in 14 days with ease – even if you have no list, no budget and no name on the market" http://www.onlinebizwiz.com/lbvideos/

Jeff Herring

Jeff Herring has a special offer for you, free templates to make your content creation and article writing much quicker and easier.
http://jeffherring.com/stop-that-template

Carla McNeil

Get free report on, "7 Facebook Rules That Could Ruin Your Business"

http://clickherenow.co/BCSB/

Nilofer Safdar

Get free report – Discover How You Can Become A Bestselling Author Like I Did, By Taking Advantage Of A "Shortcut" Opportunity That I Have For You http://ic.instantcustomer.com/gov3/132610/

More Client Attraction?

If you have an article that you feel belongs to a future volume of Cracking The Client Attraction Code, we invite you to contact us.

Carla McNeil & Nilofer Safdar
http://Crackingtheclientattractioncode.com
info@crackingtheclientattractioncode.com

We will make sure that you, as the author are credited for your contributions. Thank You.

And visit our website for new and updated stories not found in the hard copy of Cracking The Client Attraction Code..........the code goes on!

www.crackingtheclientattractioncode.com

You can also contact us for consulting and speaking engagements, information about our newsletters, other books, audio and video programs, workshops and training programs.

Carla McNeil & Nilofer Safdar

Lightning Source UK Ltd.
Milton Keynes UK
UKOW01f2020161017
311070UK00006B/583/P

9 780994 728500